Place-Based Education

Connecting Classrooms & Communities

by David Sobel

A publication of The Orion Society

THE ORION SOCIETY'S NATURE LITERACY SERIES offers fresh educational ideas and strategies for cultivating "nature literacy" —the ability to learn from and respond to direct experience of nature. Nature literacy is not information gathered from a series of isolated, external "facts," but a deep understanding of natural and human communities. As such, it demands a far more integrated and intimate educational approach. Nature literacy means seeing nature as a connected, inclusive whole. Furthermore, it means redefining community as an interwoven web of nature and culture, a relationship marked by mutual dependence and one enriched and sustained by love. The materials presented in this series are directed to teachers, parents, and others concerned with creating an education that nurtures informed and active stewards of the natural world.

**Place-Based Education:
Connecting Classrooms & Communities**

by David Sobel

ISBN 0-913098-55-8
ISBN 978-0-913098-55-4

The Orion Society
187 Main Street, Great Barrington, MA 01230
telephone: 413/528-4422   facsimile: 413/528-0676
email: questions@orionsociety.org
website: www.oriononline.org/education

Cover image by Clare Walker Leslie
Photographs © James Tyler and The Center for Ecoliteracy

Printed in the U.S.A. on recycled paper
3RD printing

Table of Contents

Foreword

In an increasingly globalized world, there are often pressures for communities and regions to subordinate themselves to the dominant economic models and to devalue their local cultural identity, traditions, and history in preference to a flashily marketed homogeneity. Furthermore, at a time when industrial pollution, biodiversity/habitat loss, and aquifer depletion are becoming widespread and acute, such pressures often exacerbate the problems by encouraging unsustainable patterns of consumption and land use, and by weakening familial and community relationships that are deeply tied to the local environment. A process of disintegration occurs as basic connections to the land fray and communities become less resilient and less able to deal with the dislocations that globalization and ecological deterioration bring about. A community's health—human and more-than-human—suffers.

In his recent book, *In the Presence of Fear*, Wendell Berry describes disconnections that are now familiar to many of us.

We are involved now in a profound failure of imagination. Most of us cannot imagine the wheat beyond the bread, or the farmer beyond the wheat, or the farm beyond the farmer, or the history beyond the farm. Most people cannot imagine the forest and the forest economy that produced their houses and furniture and paper; or the landscapes, the streams, and the weather that fill their pitchers and bathtubs and swimming pools with water. Most people appear to assume that when they have paid their money for these things they have entirely met their obligations.

The Orion Society has always shared Berry's belief that the path to a sane, sustainable existence must start with a fundamental reimagining of the ethical, economic, political, and spiritual foundations upon which society is based, and that this process needs to occur within the context of a deep local knowledge of place. We believe that the solutions to many of our ecological problems lie in an approach that celebrates, empowers, and nurtures the cultural, artistic, historical, and spiritual resources of each local community and region, and champions their ability to bring those resources to bear on the healing of nature and community.

Schools and other educational institutions can and should play a central role in this process, but for the most part they do not. Indeed, they have often contributed to the problem by educating young people to be, in David Orr's words, "mobile, rootless and autistic toward their places." A significant transformation of education might begin with the effort to learn how events and processes close to home relate to regional, national, and global forces and events, leading to a new understanding of ecological stewardship and community. In its educational programs, The Orion Society supports the propagation of such an enlightened localism—a local/global dialectic that is sensitive to broader ecological and social relationships at the same time as it strengthens and deepens people's sense of community and land.

In the early 1990s, The Orion Society termed this pedagogical strategy a "place-based" approach to education. Since that time we have continued to foster and refine this approach through a variety of publishing materials, teacher training institutes and fellowship programs, and symposia and conferences held in collaboration with dozens of schools, universities, and governmental and nongovernmental institutions.

Place-based education might be characterized as the pedagogy of community, the reintegration of the individual into her homeground and the restoration of the essential links between a person and her place. In the years since we embarked on these efforts, we have seen place-based education emerge as a flourishing phenomenon across the continent, adapting to and evolving from the uniqueness of each community where it has been used.

In practice, place-based education often belies the seriousness of the ecological problems it seeks to remedy because it emphasizes creative exploration and the joyful realization of the ties that connect a person with nature and culture in her place. It does so out of the realization that love—love of nature, love of one's neighbors and community—is a prime motivating factor in personal transformation, and the transformation of culture. Place-based education pioneer Dr.

John Elder of Middlebury College comments on this in his foreword to *Stories in the Land: A Place-Based Education Anthology*:

> *An approach to education that begins with love is a romantic pedagogy. It is opposed to the classical, or deductive, model that impresses knowledge, in the different cookie-cutters of each discipline, on the amorphous mind and sensibilities of children and the otherwise insufficiently formed.... I don't mean here to value the romantic impulse exclusively, but rather to suggest that, when facing the environmental challenges of our day, it can be a helpful corrective to the hermetic tendencies within the more classical and deductive disciplines.*

Place-based education challenges the meaning of education by asking seemingly simple questions: Where am I? What is the nature of this place? What sustains this community? It often employs a process of re-storying, whereby students are asked to respond creatively to stories of their homeground so that, in time, they are able to position themselves, imaginatively and actually, within the continuum of nature and culture in that place. They become part of the community, rather than a passive observer of it.

Orion's Nature Literacy Series of books has attempted to deepen and disseminate place-based educational philosophy by offering teachers, parents, and others well-articulated reports by leading practitioners. The first volume in the series, *Beyond Ecophobia: Reclaiming the Heart in Nature Education* by David Sobel, is widely regarded as a seminal text for the teaching of environmental education at the elementary school level.

This new book by Dr. Sobel is the most comprehensive review of place-based education to be published, an eloquent layering of pedagogy and practical examples taken from practicing classrooms—urban, suburban, and rural, coast-to-coast. *Place-Based Education: Connecting Classrooms & Communities* offers scientific and anecdotal evidence that place-based education is successfully meeting, and in many cases, surpassing the various standards and mandates that are increasingly a part of educational reform in this country.

According to Sobel, place-based education is not simply a way to integrate the curriculum around a study of place, but a means of inspiring stewardship and an authentic renewal and revitalization of civic life. In a youth culture shaped by the mall, an education that values local distinctiveness and richness stands as a patch of wildness amid a growing expanse of tarmac. Sobel celebrates this wildness, explaining that place-based education's "practitioners draw strength from the image of those hearty dandelions and other herbaceous plants that force their way up through asphalt."

"Drops of waters and rootlets unite!" he declares. "Give me your students yearning to be free! It's a simple proposition really. Bring education back into the neighborhood."

—Laurie Lane-Zucker
Executive Director, January 2004

Place-Based Education

Connecting Classrooms & Communities

Something's Happening Here

As you stroll down the halls of your neighborhood school at nine o'clock on a Wednesday morning, you notice that something seems odd. Many of the classrooms are empty, you realize; the students are not in their places with bright, shiny faces. Where are they? If you could cast your gaze out beyond the school walls, across the community, you'd find them. In the town wood lot, a forester teaches tenth graders which trees should be marked for an upcoming thinning project. Downtown, a group of middle school students are collecting water samples in an urban stream to determine if there's enough dissolved oxygen to support reintroduced trout. Out on the school grounds, a few children are sitting on benches writing poems while another group works with a landscape architect and the math teacher to create a map that will be used to plan the schoolyard garden. Inside, in one of the full classrooms, eighth graders are working with second graders to teach them about the history of the local Cambodian community. In the cafeteria, the city solid-waste manager is consulting with a group of fifth graders and the school lunch staff to help them design the recycling and composting program. No, those bright shiny faces aren't sitting behind desks—they are all around the school, and out in the schoolyard and the community, learning in a whole new way.

You don't have to pinch yourself. It's not a dream. Place-based education is taking root in urban and rural, northern and southern, well-to-do and rough-around-the-edges schools and communities across the country. Take a whirlwind tour with me as we drop in on some of these happenings.

Two recent headlines in the Littleton, New Hampshire, *Courier* paint the picture: "Using the River as a Textbook" and "The Town Becomes the Classroom." Like many small New England cities, Littleton had turned its back on its downtown river, the Ammonusuc, at the end of the nineteenth century. Now, with funding from the Department of Transportation, the town is creating a Riverwalk, which will connect Main Street with the river and open up a new economic development zone. Working in conjunction with the town planner and the town engineer, teachers and community members are engaging students in the design of a river museum at one end of the Riverwalk. Different grades will be responsible for the changing exhibitions in the museum. High school history students might create an exhibit on logging history in the Great Northern Forest. Sixth grade science students will design hands-on water testing activities. Perhaps third graders will take on the task of creating the entrance mural as part of their study of local plants and animals.

The town is already functioning as a classroom in a novel collaboration between Chutter's General Store and the marketing program at the Littleton High School's vocational center. When the well-established downtown candy store realized that its internet sales site was costing more than the revenues it generated, the owners looked to the school for a solution. At the same time, the high school needed more space and the marketing class was seeking real-world projects. So the school district and the town agreed to rehabilitate a space below the candy store to create a marketing classroom in exchange for students participating in reviving Chutter's internet business. By having the marketing class take over the website, the students get economics experience while the candy store owners generate a bit of revenue as a result of the reduced labor costs.

Through a balanced focus on economic development and environmental preservation, the community and its businesses get revitalized, state curriculum standards are met, and students are given invaluable opportunities to learn in real-world settings.

In Louisiana, getting out of the classroom often means getting into mosquitoes, so the 4H Club at Caldwell Middle School in Terrebonne Parish took on the practical challenge of mosquito control. One parent, whose daughter has asthma, suggested that they try to find a way to control mosquitoes in residential areas without aerial spraying of pesticides. Students and teachers accepted this challenge and began their study by raising guppies to see if they would eat mosquito larvae. But these students got a lesson in ecology when a professor from Nichols State University recommended native mosquito fish instead, because of the problems caused when nonnative species are introduced into local waters. So the students turned their attention to the mosquito fish, breeding and then releasing them into stagnant ponds, ditches, and even swimming pools. According to Melynda Rodrigue, 4H sponsor and Caldwell teacher, the project branched in multiple directions. Math students charted the numbers of mosquito fish offspring and the time period needed to repopulate the tanks; science classes studied the fish's life cycle; and social studies classes examined the impact on the community's environment. Some students used their writing skills to create a brochure for distribution to the community, while others got public speaking experience through presentations at neighboring schools.

In Berkeley, California, a similar grassroots school-and-community effort has transformed into a bioregional initiative. One vegetable garden at the Martin Luther King Middle School gave rise to the idea of having a garden on every schoolyard in Berkeley, which evolved into the dream of a garden on every schoolyard in California. And since all the children in any one school can't be fed with produce from a single garden, connections between local farmers and the school district were forged. Instead of freeze-dried burritos trucked in from the Midwest, how about burritos with organic beans and cheese grown and produced by area farmers who are threatened by suburban sprawl? These ideas led to the creation of the Food Systems Project, whose goal is to have all the food in the Berkeley school lunch program be organic and locally grown within the next decade while also making food preparation and agriculture education an integral part of each school's curriculum.

The Food Systems Project is funded by the United States Department of Agriculture's Linking Farms to Schools initiative, the California Department of Health, and the Center for Ecoliteracy, a broad coalition of funders trying to address the problems of child nutrition, school improvement, and sustainable agriculture in an integrated fashion. Project director Janet Brown comments:

> *By using food as an organizing principle for systemic change, the program addresses the root causes of poor academic performance, psychosocial*

behavior disorders, and escalating children's health issues such as obesity, asthma and diabetes. At the same time the program connects the loss of farmland and farming as a way of life and the social problems facing school communities. (Sobel, 2001).

Doesn't it make sense—using the daily meal as a focal point for learning?

Comenius, the seventeenth-century education philosopher, articulated one of the core precepts of place-based education when he said, "Knowledge of the nearest things should be acquired first, then that of those farther and farther off." (Woodhouse, 2001) You can't really get much nearer than the internal microenvironment of your digestive system as a focal point for the curriculum. The mosquito-breeding ponds in your backyard and the downtown places where you shop are similarly appropriate contexts for learning. And so, as the rallying cry for place-based educators, I nominate that popular Beatles refrain, "Get back. Get back. Get back to where you once belonged."

Distance from Beauty

If we're going to get back, we need to look first at where we are now.

Katie Avery, third grade teacher in the White Mountain–encircled town of Gorham, New Hampshire, got at the crux of the problem during a curriculum planning meeting when she asked, "Why are we using textbooks that focus on landforms in Arizona when we have such amazing resources right in our backyard?" Good question. Gorham sits in the shadow of Mount Washington, the loftiest peak in New England, and home to the worst weather in the world. The Presidential Range has a fascinating alpine zone, classic glacial cirques, and some of the most awe-inspiring mountain terrain in the country. Yet most of the students have never hiked the mountains and the curriculum ignores this great local teaching resource. Instead, geography is taught using pretty pictures of faraway places. Generic textbooks designed for the big markets of California and Texas provide the same homogenized, un-nutritious diet as all those fast-food places on the strip. State-mandated curriculum and high-stakes tests put everyone on the same page on the same day and discourage an attention to significant nearby learning opportunities. Educational biodiversity falls prey to the bulldozers of standardization. Schools hover like alien spacecraft, luring children away from their home communities. More and more, we drive a wedge between our children and the tangible beauty of the real world. The landscape of schooling looks like American urban sprawl.

In the provocatively titled article "How My Schooling Taught Me Contempt for the Earth," Bill Bigelow illustrates this alienation. During his boyhood in the late 1950s, he rambled the hills around his home in Tiburon, California, just across the bridge from San Francisco.

I loved the land. I spent every after-school moment and every weekend or summer day, outside until it got dark. I knew where to dig the best underground forts and how to avoid the toffee-like clay soil.... I knew from long observation at nearby ponds the exact process of a pollywog's transition into a frog, and the relative speed of different kinds of snakes: garter vs. gopher vs. western racer.... [We also] had a love/hate relationship with "development." Almost as another natural habitat, we played in the houses under construction: hide and seek, climbing and jumping off roofs, and rafting in basements when they flooded.

Located near wetlands, grasslands, remnant redwood forests, and new development, his school was well situated for field trips and for social and natural science learning.

*How did our schooling extend or suppress our naive earth-knowledge and our love of place? Through silence about the earth and the native people of Tiburon, Bel-Aire School, perched on the slopes of a steep golden-grassed hill, taught plenty. We actively learned to **not-think** about the earth, about that place where we were. We could have been anywhere—or nowhere. Teachers made no effort to incorporate our vast, if immature, knowledge of the land into the curriculum. Whether it was in the study of history, writing, science, arithmetic, reading or art, school erected a Berlin*

Wall between academics and the rest of our lives.... The hills above the school were a virtual wilderness of grasslands and trees, but in six years, I can't recall a single "field trip" to the wide-open spaces right on our doorstep. We became inured to spending days in manufactured space, accustomed to watching more earth bulldozed and covered with yet more manufactured spaces. (Bigelow, 1996)

It was the same everywhere. In my mid-twenties, I became interested in plant taxonomy. After peering at a violet under a hand lens one afternoon, I paged through *Gray's Manual of Botany* trying to understand the difference between stamens, pistils, and calyxes, when poof! the proverbial light bulb went on. In my mind's eye, I saw the much-larger-than-life-size model of a flower that had perched on the lab table at the front left corner of my tenth grade biology classroom. *"That was a model of flowers that grew right outside the classroom door!"* I said to myself in disbelief. As a high school biology student, my unquestioned misconception was that this was a model of a rainforest flower, or at least a far-away flower. It never occurred to me that real flowers, with real flower parts, existed on the school playground. Yet, I was your true science geek—carried a slide rule, got over 700 on my biology achievement test, and planned on following Martin Arrowsmith's footsteps into biochemical research. I was on the ball, but most of our teachers had no sense that it was important to connect up the classroom world with the nearby outside world.

Place-based education is the antidote to the not-thinking about the Earth common in many schools. Instead of settling for textbook accounts of distant places, Katie Avery and the other third grade teachers and students at Edward Fenn Elementary School worked with a children's book author to write and illustrate a book about Gorham. As you read it, you'll "laugh at the hilarious adventures of Peewee Skunk, Amos Moose and Shylee Beaver, go back in time and learn about the history of Gorham, visit different places around Gorham today, and find out about the jobs people do." (From the back cover of the book.) Is it a surprise that the third grade social studies test scores and civic pride increased as a result of this project?

Such a project is a perfect segue into offering up a definition of place-based education:

Place-based education is the process of using the local community and environment as a starting point to teach concepts in language arts, mathematics, social studies, science, and other subjects across the curriculum. Emphasizing hands-on, real-world learning experiences, this approach to education increases academic achievement, helps students develop stronger

© James Tyler/Center for Ecoliteracy

Emphasizing hands-on, real-world learning experiences, this approach to education increases academic achievement, helps students develop stronger ties to their community, enhances students' appreciation for the natural world, and creates a heightened commitment to serving as active, contributing citizens.

ties to their community, enhances students' appreciation for the natural world, and creates a heightened commitment to serving as active, contributing citizens. Community vitality and environmental quality are improved through the active engagement of local citizens, community organizations, and environmental resources in the life of the school.

Place-based education converts the activist plaint of Not in My Backyard (NIMBY) to Please in my Backyard (PIMBY). Please in my Backyard means that schooling should start out the back door with a focus on the neighborhood rather than the solar system in the early grades. As a truly grassroots movement, its practitioners draw strength from the image of those hearty dandelions and other herbaceous plants that force their way up through asphalt. As William James described:

> *I am done with great things and big things, great institutions and big success, and I am for those tiny, invisible, molecular moral forces that work from individual to individual by creeping through the crannies of the world like so many rootlets, or like the capillary oozing of water, yet which, if you give them time, will rend the hardest monuments of man's pride. (James, 1899)*

Drops of waters and rootlets unite! Give me your students yearning to be free! It's a simple proposition really. Bring education back into the neighborhood. Connect students with adult mentors, conservation commissions, and local businesses. Get teachers and students into the community, into the woods, and on the streets—closer to beauty and true grit. Get the town engineer, the mayor, and the environmental educators onto the schoolyard and inside the four walls of the school. These are the places we all belong.

Reconceptualizing Environmental Education

I suspect you're wondering, how does "place-based education" differ from "environmental education"? Many educators are ready to move beyond environmental education, feeling that the term is too narrow and carries too much baggage. Environmental education grew out of the Nature Studies movement of the early twentieth century and traditionally focused on learning about the natural sciences—field ecology, nutrient cycles, plant and animal taxonomy. But in recent years, environmental education evolved into issues and catastrophe education—learning about rainforest destruction, ozone depletion, toxic waste, and endangered species. Place-based education takes us back to basics, but in a broader and more inclusive fashion. Desirable environmental education, or what we're calling place-based education, teaches about both the natural and built environments. The history, folk culture, social problems, economics, and aesthetics of the community and its environment are all on the agenda. In fact, one of the core objectives is to look at how landscape, community infrastructure, watersheds, and cultural traditions all interact and shape each other.

This inclusive view of environmental education is well articulated in Roger Hart's book *Children's Participation: The Theory and Practice of Involving Young Citizens in Community Development and Environmental Care.* With examples from Asia, Africa, Europe, and North and South America, Hart illustrates how education and initiatives in resource protection together form the heart of the movement to develop sustainable communities.

> *Environmental education must be radically reconceived in order to be seen as fundamental to the residents of communities from all social classes in all countries. We need programmes based on the identification and investigation of problems by residents themselves, with "action research" as the dominant methodology. There is of course a central place for the teaching of environmental science—"ecology" as it is often called—but this should at first be directly related to the local environment. Environmental education from this perspective is intrinsically tied to community development in general. (Hart, 1997)*

Hart's charge to educators is echoed in *Closing the Achievement Gap*, which describes the results of a nationwide study by the State Education and Environment Roundtable (SEER). SEER researchers identified schools in twelve states that were using this reconceptualized form of environmental education, describing it as "using the environment as an integrating context," or EIC-based learning. In this report, researchers Gerald Lieberman and Linda Hoody explain that:

> *EIC-based learning is not primarily focused on learning about the environment nor is it limited to developing environmental awareness. It is about using a school's surroundings and community as a framework within which students can construct their own learning, guided by teachers and administrators using proven educational practices....*

David Sobel

Since the ecosystems surrounding schools and their communities vary as dramatically as the nation's landscape, the term environment may mean different things at every school; it may be a river, a forest, a city park, or a garden carved out of an asphalt playground. In creating an EIC curriculum, educators have the opportunity to define the local environment broadly, to encompass natural ecosystems and sociocultural systems in their community. Each school, by necessity, therefore designs its own program independently to take into account their specific locale, resources and student needs. (Lieberman and Hoody, 1998)

Hart, Lieberman, and Hoody are all advocating for a kind of educational "speciation." Think about Darwin's finches in the Galapagos Islands. Darwin's ideas about evolution and natural selection were significantly shaped by his realization that the islands were populated with an array of finch species. He noticed that different islands with different ecosystems supported finches with varying body sizes, beaks, and plumage. Therefore, he speculated that one species of finch had arrived in the Galapagos long ago and that all the different species had evolved as the finches adapted to the different food sources, perching opportunities, and potential predators of each island. On islands with abundant seed sources, a species developed with a short, thick seed-crushing bill. On other islands with abundant flying insects, a species evolved with thin bills and a movement repertoire adapted for snatching insects out of the air.

Schools, I'm suggesting, should be encouraged to evolve in similar ways. If teachers and administrators are attentive to the particularities of place, climate, community organizations, environmental learning centers, and parental concerns, then unique species of curriculum and project-based learning will evolve. For instance, when a community forum in Antrim, New Hampshire, found that citizens were concerned about the condition of downtown Memorial Park, fifth grade teacher Barbara Black and sixth grade teacher Letitia Rice took on a full-year project to revitalize the park. The cultural and environmental parameters of the project included the park committee's interest in replacing exotics with native species, the sixth grade curriculum focus on plant science, and the teachers' interest in taking on a real, community-based problem. Students mapped the park, identified existing flora, researched native flora, came up with proposals for a landscape design, made presentations to town committees, and finally implemented the planting scheme in the late spring. It was a successful synthesis of meeting a community need and addressing the district and state curriculum guidelines.

Curriculum speciation also evolved in the interdisciplinary STREAMS program at the Huntingdon, Pennsylvania, area middle school. Water quality tests conducted by middle school students at Muddy Run, a local stream, indicated abnormally high levels of bacteria. Through collaboration with local college professors and students, the middle school students identified the crumbling municipal sewer system as a probable major cause of the contamination. What started out as a science curriculum project turned into an integrated writing and social action initiative as students and teachers mounted a campaign to convince community members of the seriousness of the problem. The end result was a $250,000 grant from the Pennsylvania Infrastructure Investment Authority to repair the municipal sewer system. (Lieberman and Hoody, 1998)

Instead of being constricted by standardized curriculum guidelines (isn't that one possible outcome of the recent No Child Left Behind legislation that mandates national testing from grades three through eight?), these teachers in New Hampshire and Pennsylvania allowed speciation to occur. By adapting their curriculum to the local conditions, they allowed completely different and unique learning "finches" to evolve. And by becoming players in the community ecosystem, these teachers and students acted back on the system, improving the health of the environment and fulfilling community dreams.

What's emerging here is a "pedagogy of place," a theoretical framework that emphasizes the necessary interpenetration of school, community, and environment, whether it's urban, suburban, or rural. In *Living and Learning in Rural Communities*, an evaluation report on the Annenberg Rural Challenge Program, Vito Perrone and the other authors take a stab at articulating the uniqueness of place-based education. Just as curriculum undergoes speciation when it adapts to local conditions, educational theory undergoes speciation when it tries to make sense of the conditions that allow new finches to take wing.

*Another way to think about this focus on place is to understand that a "grounded" or "rooted" learner stands **within** the world, acting on its many elements, rather than standing outside looking in, acting in large measure as an observer, which is the typical stance expected of students in schools. What* *is notable from our close observations of student work that has an embedded quality—meaning that the student is in the community, researching aspects of its history, learning about local lore, researching and reconstructing aspects of a local watershed, conducting community health surveys, developing exhibits for the local museum—is that the quality of the work deepens greatly, is more carefully attended to, assumes genuine meaning.*

*Students easily distinguish this rooted work from typical work in which they stand outside. A grounded, rooted learner understands that his/her actions matter, that they affect the community beyond the school. It is out of this particular formulation that the "**student as resource to the community**" takes shape—that understanding that students need to be thought of as productive assets to the health of a community. A pedagogy of place, then, recontextualizes education locally. It makes education a preparation for citizenship, both locally and in wider contexts, while also providing the basis for continuing scholarship. (Rural Challenge Research and Evaluation Program, 1999)*

The new idea here is that we're not preparing students for tomorrow, we're preparing them to solve the problems of today. You don't learn about ecology so you can help protect nature in the future. You learn so you can make a difference here and now.

Out Behind Taco Bell

In Keene, New Hampshire, the heart of the region where I live and teach, one of our attempts to act on this "student-as-resource-to-the-community" idea is the Rachel Marshall Outdoor Learning Laboratory (RMOLL) project. Under the inspired guidance of project directors Bo Hoppin and Paul Bocko, RMOLL is a collaboration between the Friends of the Ashuelot River Park, the Keene public schools, the city parks and recreation department, and Antioch New England Graduate School. Since the project's inception in 1995, a neglected tract of weedy forest has become a model of community partnership.

The initial idea in 1995 was simple: Develop a three-acre tract of land into a learning laboratory for the local five elementary schools, middle school, and high school. Concurrently, the city government was interested in reviving the untended riparian corridor along the Ashuelot River as a city park. And soon after work began on the learning lab, a number of local foundations bought a defunct gas station next to the Taco Bell and began transforming it into an elegant, landscaped gateway to the river park. The existence of the learning lab helped support the funding for the gateway, and vice versa—an example of the synergy between place-based education and community development.

One of the strategies was to treat the schools as architectural subcontractors. Hoppin and Bocko identified tasks that needed to be accomplished, and then we asked teachers to submit proposals to work on these projects. For instance, some fifth grade classes took up the challenge of converting a section of gravelly road into indigenous wildlife habitat. Groups of students took on sections of the area, worked with a landscape designer, and installed a variety of native plants. Another project was a competition to come up with a design for a wildlife observation station and a gateway for the side entrance to the park. Teams of seventh graders (involving 175 students) created models and posters of their proposals, which were evaluated and voted on by their peers. Simultaneously, a group of high school students weighed the pros and cons of building a boardwalk through one of the seasonally wet sections of the land. Their study involved answering questions such as whether "the boardwalk would help or hinder younger students in immersing themselves in nature study at the site."

Once a critical mass of teachers was interested in the project, the next step was to create a new class in our environmental studies program at Antioch New England called Environmental Education in the Public Schools. The core objective was to have graduate students work with middle-school teachers and students on RMOLL-related projects. This provided hands-on learning for graduate students in shaping hands-on learning for the middle school curriculum. At Keene High School, RMOLL and the broader Ashuelot River Park became a major focus for the new Advanced Placement Environmental Studies course. High school students investigated the endangered dwarf wedge mussel population in the river and collected oral histories from older local residents regarding river life before the construction of the Army Corps of Engineers dam upstream.

A summer camp program for middle schoolers now focuses on the full length of the Ashuelot River from high in the New Hampshire hills more than seventy miles down to its confluence with the Connecticut River. And summer institutes for Keene public school teachers ensure a steady flow of recruits to design new projects. In the last few years, the focus has moved from the learning lab to the whole river park to all of the different city-owned parcels of land. The *Keene Sentinel*, the local daily, recently initiated "Tracing Places," a weekly column on historical and environmental sites in the city, written by students. The series not only brings attention to the city's conservation land, but is also integrated with the high school American studies curriculum. The column recently won the New England Newspapers Award for the best community engagement project by a daily paper for papers of all sizes in New England.

Just as the mycelial threads of a fungus creep outward and weave together the detritus on the forest floor, the RMOLL project has woven together numerous elements of our small city. At the dedication ceremony for the laboratory, Hannah Jacobs, a high school student from the Advanced Placement Environmental Studies class, gave one of the speeches. She described the educational virtue of the lab saying:

> *The laboratory is truly a little natural world in the midst of bustling Keene. It is amazing to experience the peace of a forest with cars, horns, and sirens all blaring in the distance. When I was doing research here for my biology project, I stood in awe as I watched a Cooper's hawk hunting chickadees for a noonday snack. Math classes have measured the slope of the land, art and archeology classes at the high school have researched the park's history, and writing classes have sat here to compose pieces with inspiration from nature.*

But then she reached beyond her own experience, beyond the classroom, to describe the broader meaning of the program.

> *I think the most incredible aspect of the laboratory is its level of community and student involvement. Many students are scared and upset when they see the natural landscape changing around them. We feel like we have no voice in the development of our community, and decisions that are*

made by the leaders about economic development do affect us significantly and change the character of Keene. The Learning Laboratory actually gave us a chance to make a positive impact and have our voices heard. We were participating in the preservation of a piece of land in our town and deciding how that land would be managed. How refreshing it is to have our suggestions and input listened to, acknowledged, and implemented.

On the banks of the Ashuelot River, those molecular moral forces of place-based education are creeping through the crannies in the very soil, creating a rich compost of students, citizens, and sustainability. While across the country, similar grassroots initiatives are preparing the ground for something even bigger.

New Directions in School Reform

A pamphlet describing the innovative School on the River program in Lacrosse, Wisconsin, reads:

> *Changing a public school has never been an easy task, however Longfellow Middle School's "School on a River" program has proven it can be done. The process of creating a successful middle level program like School on a River is different from traditional public education.... School on a River is a long term commitment to actively involve students in learning within the school, environment and community.... Students are in a collaborative enterprise with their teachers, community, government, and environment that will prepare them to become active participants in the future.*

More and more, place-based education is becoming the model for school reform efforts. The Rural School and Community Trust, SEER's Model Schools program, Chesapeake Bay Foundation's Bay Schools Project, and many charter schools have a place-based education paradigm at their core. Because the underlying mindsets of these place-based programs are really quite different, it's important to differentiate them from the more narrow-minded school reform initiatives that have spread their kudzu-like tendrils across the public school landscape in recent decades. Let's examine some of the new philosophical directions that characterize a place-based model for school reform.

New Direction #1: From Extraction to Sustainability as the Underlying Metaphor

Many of today's school-reform initiatives threaten to create "reform schools," those places where we used to send delinquent youth. These were basically lock-ups, offering education behind bars with an emphasis on strict discipline and rote memorization. Similarly, the cultural literacy and high-stakes standards movements threaten to lock the school doors and throw away the key. They want to increase seat time, the consumption of decontextualized facts, and test scores. The effect is to separate students from the community, from their inner selves, and from the real world. Joseph Kiefer and Martin Kemple of the Foodworks Program in Vermont take this characterization of reform efforts a few steps further.

> *School reform movements sweep the country every ten or fifteen years or so, purportedly to address perennial questions about the relevance and accountability of our educational system. From years of working in public schools, we have become convinced that most contemporary school restructuring efforts—be they called 'systemic school change' or 'standards-based education'—are essentially programs for retooling students to become efficient workers, designed to make children more competitive in the national economy, or more recently, in the emerging global economy. Absent from the debates nationally and locally about our educational system has been critical discourse on the responsibility of schools to the communities that support them and to the planet's life-support systems. (Kiefer and Kemple, 1999)*

Traditional school-reform initiatives are grounded in the paradigm of limitless resources and "the purposes of an extractive economy determined to dominate nature and increase the material wealth and security of our own species." (Smith and Williams, 1999, quoting Berry) Instead, we need a school-reform model that focuses on the principle of sustainability—figuring out how to live within our means at both a local and global level. Embracing sustainability as an organizing principle means that we accept a concept of limited resources and start to look for ways to simultaneously enhance economic vitality, environmental quality, and school improvement at the local level. And it means facing the challenges of environmental preservation, school and terrorist violence, and community health in age-appropriate ways within the school curriculum.

In Lubec, Maine, the easternmost community in the United States, Lubec High School students are working hard to revitalize their community. This centuries-old fishing community has faced hard times in the last two decades as traditional fish stocks have dwindled. To keep fishing alive and to keep the local cannery open, fishermen and students have turned to aquaculturing new, marketable fish products. With support from the Rural School and Community Trust and town funding, the school has created an aquaculture study facility where students and teachers can research new techniques. One description of the project offers details:

> *Students study the life cycle of organisms and how to raise species and bring them to market; they research solutions to actual problems. They raise salmon and sea urchins, sell baitfish during ice-fishing season, and culture freshwater species like rainbow trout….*
>
> *Hank Spence, who directs Peacock Canning's special projects hatchery, has taken a keen interest in the school program, inviting students to share his research and even conduct it along with him. He is asking students to research the optimum stocking densities for raising different species and the most effective micro-algae for feeding the growing shellfish larvae. In his column in the local paper, Spence keeps the community informed of the student's work. (Bartsch, 1999)*

The students' work in Lubec connects to the Maine Learning Results, the state's curriculum guidelines, through providing contextualized learning in biology and chemistry. It also contributes to the economic revitalization of the town and prevents further depletion of native fish stocks by providing alternative work for local fishermen.

In Oakland, California, students of the Media Academy at Fremont High School are directly responsible for publishing the school newspaper, yearbook, and a community newspaper, and for producing many local public-service announcements. The Academy serves students with academic promise who were identified in junior high as potential dropouts, giving them a vision of possible employment. Local media professionals help to teach some of the classes, and internships are available for students.

> *Young people who often believe that good jobs are simply unattainable because of who they are and where they live come to see that work worthy of their desire is within their reach.... Seeing this has led to dramatic shifts in engagement and achievement and...many now graduate from high school and go on to community colleges or universities. (Smith, 2002)*

These real-world projects make the lives of the students and their community more sustainable through enhancing employment opportunities and developing a sense of commitment in students to cultural vitality.

New Direction #2: From Fragmentation to Systems Thinking as a Conceptual Model

The Oakland example above not only illustrates how place-based education fosters community ties, but also how place-based educators aspire to address the problem of alienation from school. John Goodlad estimates that two-thirds of all high school students are alienated by the education system (Chin, 2001). Perhaps they can't see the relevance of quadratic equations, Shakespeare, and the Kansas-Nebraska Act in everyday life? John Dewey had this figured out almost a hundred years ago, when he wrote in *School and Society*:

> *From the standpoint of the child, the great waste in the school comes from his inability to utilize the experiences he gets outside the school in any complete and free way within the school itself; while, on the other hand, he is unable to apply in daily life what he is learning at school. That is the isolation of the school—its isolation from life. When the child gets into the schoolroom, he has to put out of his mind a large part of the ideas, interest and activities that predominate in his home and neighborhood. So the school, being unable to utilize this everyday experience, sets painfully to work...to arouse in the child an interest in social studies. (Dewey, 1891)*

This fragmentation of the school from the community is mirrored in the fragmented curriculum. Not only is the math curriculum not connected to shopping at the local Piggly Wiggly supermarket, it's not connected to the history or art curricula in any programmatic way. Place-based educators want to advocate for an integrated curriculum that emphasizes project-based learning, teacher collabora-

© James Tyler/Center for Ecoliteracy

Eventually, the students saw their two-year project lead to the town's installation of a new water system, which resulted in an improvement in community health.

tion, and extensive use of community resources and volunteers.

When students in Parrish, Alabama, discovered high concentrations of lead in the school and then the town water supply, local chemistry teachers developed a hands-on curriculum around the issue. But what started out as chemistry curriculum slid sideways into neurophysiology when looking at lead and learning disabilities, and then ultimately evolved into social studies and economics when the students got involved in town politics. The research that began in the school moved out into the community and spurred interactions with county health officials, engineers, and local biologists. Eventually, the students saw their two-year project lead to the town's installation of a new water system, which resulted in an improvement in community health. Through this kind of project, students can start to understand how the educational, economic, and health branches of the community are systemically related to each other, rather than stand-alone entities.

New Direction #3: From Here-and-Now to Long-Ago-and-Far-Away as a Developmental Guideline for Curriculum Design

A third conviction of community and place-based education reformers is to undergird school change with a commitment to developmental appropriateness. Just as we wait until fifth or sixth grade to introduce explicit sex education in the classroom, it seems wise to hold off on rainforest education until the students have a solid understanding of the temperate hardwoods forest on the edge of the playground. Oberlin College professor and author David Orr suggests:

> *We all have an affinity for the natural world, what the Harvard biologist Edward O. Wilson calls "biophilia." This tug toward life is strongest at an early age, when we are most alert and impressionable. Before their minds have been marinated in the culture of television, consumerism, shopping malls, computers, and freeways, children can find magic in trees, water, animals, landscapes, and their own places. Properly cultivated and validated by caring and knowledgeable adults, fascination with nature can mature into ecological literacy and eventually into more purposeful lives. (Center for Ecoliteracy, 2000)*

My own research in the development of children's relationship with nature resonates with Orr's contention that there is a sensitive period during the elementary years when children are predisposed to bond with the nearby natural world. (Sobel, 1996) It makes developmental sense to progress from near to far—to use the schoolyard, the neighborhood, and the adjacent marshlands as the context for learning in kindergarten through sixth grade. It's the Russian nesting dolls model of curriculum development.

Of course, current practices tend in the opposite direction. In order to provide more time on-task, recess is being eliminated at many schools. And even when recess is allowed, it commonly occurs on sterile, asphalt-covered schoolyards filled with manufactured play equipment, rather than in naturalized environments. Far too often field trips involve loading kids on buses and taking them to museums or zoos in nearby cities, rather than strolling through town to the local conservation area or town park. Inside the classroom, the curriculum jumps on that aforementioned spacecraft and quickly moves into outer space—literally. Have you noticed how the study of the solar system has gradually crept downward to earlier and earlier grades just as formal reading instruction has sneaked into the kindergarten? I'm anxiously awaiting a good explanation of why it's important for second graders to know the order of the planets from Mercury to Pluto. Wouldn't it be more useful to develop a solid understanding of the geography of the town the second grader lives in? And, if we're not off in outer space, we're studying Egypt or Columbus rather than the Vietnamese community two blocks down the street from the school.

The Adventure Education curriculum at The College School of Webster Groves, a K–8 independent school near St. Louis, is a perfect example of a sound developmental approach to geography, science, and social studies education. Outdoor adventures begin in kindergarten with the annual Day in the Woods, when the children study pond water, climb hills, and complete a half-mile hike. The first grader's one-night camping trip in a county park includes a ten-foot rock climb, a creek exploration, and fossil hunting. The second graders explore caves, and by third grade students go on a three-day wilderness camping trip. In fourth and fifth grade, they move backward in time, staging a historical re-enactment of a pioneer camp at an old prairie homestead. They also explore Missouri caves in earnest and recreate Tom Sawyer's and Becky's experience of sleeping in a cave overnight.

Sixth graders do a five-day wilderness trip in a national forest complete with an overnight solo—a true rite of passage for many young adolescents. Seventh graders explore the urban environment, using local transportation, sleeping in churches, performing community service, and delving into ethnic neighborhoods. By eighth grade, students travel to Okefenokee Swamp in Georgia and the southern mountains for bicycling, canoeing, and orienteering. They also conduct four days of community research in a historical Appalachian village. This movement from close and familiar to distant and strange accurately mirrors the developmental transitions unfolding in the child's psyche. When Jan Phillips, the school's director, explained the curriculum chart to me for the first time, I had one of those *ah-ha!* moments. It made so much sense! Why is this not done at more schools?

New Direction #4: From Mandated Monoculture to Emergent Diversity as a School District Goal

Finally, the character of the local environment and culture should inform the culture of the curriculum. Place-based educators tend to be queasy about mandated curriculum and high-stakes testing. Let's be clear that we're convinced that good place-based education leads to increased academic achievement (lots more on this later), but an emphasis on everybody being on the same page on the same day will severely hamper schools' abilities to be particularized or adapted to their local communities. Steve Levy, in his wonderful book *Starting from Scratch*, describes his transformation as a fourth grade teacher when he realized that if he tried to meet all his children's needs, he was doomed to failure. Addressing and remediating all of the deficits of each child was just too big a task. Instead, he decided to focus on uncovering and cultivating each child's unique genius. Helping each child identify and cultivate her inherent strengths was, he realized, an achievable goal. (Levy, 1999)

Similarly, I advocate that each school aspires to uncover and cultivate the unique genius of the local environment and community through the school's curriculum. The "genius" could be the Yup'ik culture in the Alaskan village of Kasigluk, or plays about the old-growth Blanton Forest in Harlan County, Kentucky, or GIS mapping of good salmon habitat in Seaside, Oregon. Through such work, a commitment to developing a common set of values and skills will still prevail. But recognizing that there are many interesting ways to go from point A to point B will free up teachers and schools to plan their own itinerary—and their students' will only benefit from such grounded and relevant teachings.

I am indebted to Paul Krapfel's wonderful essay "Deepening Children's Participation through Local Ecological Investigation" for this last principle. He demonstrates his leaning toward the William James's theory of change (those oozing droplets of water) when he says:

> *I have come to believe that the true path of environmental education lies not in changing the mandates, frameworks, curriculum standards, and generic textbooks but in changing the educational structure that currently expends its energy in creating mandates, frameworks, curriculum standards, and generic textbooks. Rather than requiring all teachers to teach environmental education, I would rather give teachers the freedom to teach from their hearts and give parents the freedom to choose the teaching approach they want for their children. I then want to help develop and demonstrate that an education that studies the world right around us is superior to a standardized, generic education. If we can demonstrate this convincingly, then there will be a growing demand from parents for teachers who teach this way. (Smith and Williams, 1999)*

So there are your marching orders. As teachers, make your students' experience so good that parents won't tolerate boring textbooks. As parents, ask why your child isn't involved in real-world projects. As administrators, encourage teachers to create partnerships with the local police or the conservation commission. We knew we were being successful at the Great Brook Middle School in Antrim, New Hampshire, when parents started transferring children into the district and realtors commented on the increased number of families looking for homes in the area because of the school. Through honoring that old real estate mantra, "location, location, location," we can make every school a species worthy of preservation.

What Research Says: How Place-Based Education Increases Academic Achievement

This all sounds well and good, but is there any hard evidence that this stuff works? Place-based education may be responsible, ethical, and nice, but does it make a difference for students and communities? And for many school board members, administrators, and parents the foremost question is: Does place-based education increase academic performance, or to be more blunt, does it raise test scores?

Certainly, there's lots of debate over whether test scores should be the primary means for evaluating educational success, and numerous efforts are underway to develop alternative assessment strategies. But, considering the current national climate, demonstrating that place-based education can raise test scores is one effective strategy in lobbying governments, both local and national, for support in implementing this educational approach.

The initial positive findings are raising a lot of eyebrows, inspiring both education and environmental funders in public and private arenas to look for ways to support this synergy between school reform and environmental protection. For instance, in a September 2000 report from the National Environmental Education Advisory Council to the Congress assessing the status of environmental education nationally and making recommendations for future funding, the council suggests better integration of environmental education into education-reform initiatives.

> *Environmental education has the potential to significantly improve the public education system. Many of the goals championed by education reform—such as the need to strengthen interdisciplinary teaching and critical-thinking and problem-solving skills—can be effectively accomplished using environmental education as a vehicle....*
>
> *Environmental education, by its nature, draws on and impacts many disciplines, such as science, math, history, and political science. It also is readily identifiable as a critical component of citizenship education, science literacy, and career development.... Education reform can be a mechanism for giving environmental education an established place in the curriculum, making it less subject to funding priority shifts and more likely to be a focus in teacher training. (MacKinnon, 2000)*

There are some good efforts in evaluation underway, and here's what they're finding out.

Closing the Achievement Gap: The SEER Report

The State Education and Environment Roundtable (SEER) is a cooperative endeavor of education agencies from sixteen states working to improve student learning by integrating the environment into K–12 curricula and school-reform efforts. To assess the value of these approaches, they identified model public school programs in twelve of these sixteen states and examined student behavior and performance on standardized tests at all these schools. Going into this study, people assumed that it would show increased academic performance in science, but everyone was surprised by the across-the-disciplines scope of the impact. In *Closing the Achievement Gap*, authors Lieberman and Hoody describe some of the results:

> *A recent study of 40 schools across the nation indicates that using the environment as an integrating context (EIC) in school curricula results in wide-ranging, positive effects on student learning. The study found that EIC improves student achievement in social studies, science, language arts and math. Students, teachers and administrators also reported other significant effects including: development of problem-solving, critical thinking and decision-making skills; increased enthusiasm and engagement in learning; and, gains in summative measures of educational achievement such as standardized test scores and grade point average. (Lieberman and Hoody, 1998)*

It's interesting to look at some of the details of what's happening in these schools. For instance, what do they mean when they say "increased enthusiasm and engagement in learning?" One way to quantify this increase is to look at student attendance and disciplinary referrals. In nine studies comparing EIC students to students in traditional programs in the same school, EIC students demonstrate better behavior, attendance, and attitudes than traditional students.

> *In [Dallas,] Texas, for instance, in the first year of Hotchkiss Elementary's EIC programs, teachers made 560 disciplinary referrals to the office. The next year, as program implementation expanded, the number dropped to 160. The following year, with the EIC curriculum fully established, Hotchkiss administrators reported only 50 disciplinary referrals. Both the principal and teachers attribute these decreases in behavioral problems to students' increased engagement in learning. (Lieberman and Hoody, 1998)*

At the Little Falls High School in Little Falls, Minnesota, EIC students had 54 percent fewer suspensions than other ninth graders, and at Valley High School in Louisville, Kentucky, EIC students had an 11 percent higher rate of attendance than other students. We encountered a charming example of this in Littleton, New Hampshire, this past year. The physics teacher was teaching his unit on mechanical advantage by involving students in the reconstruction of a neighborhood trail where they had to use pulleys, levers, and fulcrums to accomplish the task. On Senior Skip Day one of the students commented, "I want you to know, Mr. Church, that I skipped all the rest of my classes today, but I just couldn't miss this class. I'm too committed to what we're doing to skip this."

Quantifying attendance and behavior problems is a good way of getting at that elusive concept of motivation. Obviously, if students are more motivated, more committed to learning, then it's more likely that learning will sink in and take hold rather than evaporate. The comments from one seventh grade student at the Radnor Middle School in Wayne, Pennsylvania, make this clear.

> *I signed up for Watershed because I thought it would be easier. But let me tell you: it is a lot harder. It's fun in a way that it's harder. I actually want to learn now.... I just got awakened to the fact that I love school for the first time in seven years.*
>
> *Last year, I didn't like school. I took forever to learn. Sometimes I turned in assignments late. But now I don't because I like the overall learning experience better.... Before I studied really hard for the test, did the test, probably got an A and then I forgot everything. Now stuff is actually interesting to learn and I know that I can use it later if I get it now. (Lieberman and Hoody, 1998)*

It's not surprising that test scores increase as a function of increased enthusiasm for learning. For simplicity's sake, let's just look at language arts. Since reading scores seem to be the Holy Grail of educational reform, perhaps the EIC program can be one of the knights in shining armor. In the SEER study, seventeen comparisons of reading scores on standardized tests indicated that students in EIC programs outperform their peers in traditional programs. For instance, in Dallas at the Hotchkiss Elementary School, students showed significant increases in writing scores after the EIC programs were implemented.

The passing rates of fourth graders from the 1996–97 class, the first to learn through EIC approaches, surpassed by 13 percent those of students in the 1995–96 class. According to staff members in the Texas Education Agency's Division of Student Assessment, Hotchkiss's gains were "extremely significant" when compared to the statewide average gain of one percent during the same period. (Lieberman and Hoody, 1998)

The improvements appear to span the spectrum of language-arts assessments. Students read with improved understanding, there's more variety in their writing genres, styles, and strategies, they connect and synthesize complex ideas more effectively, and they create a greater volume of higher quality work. Finally, students speak out with increased skill and confidence. In Glenwood Springs, Colorado, the Riverwatch program in the science department at the high school engaged students in studying the relationship between land use practices and water quality. When three Riverwatch students attended a community meeting, they got drawn into speaking about the importance of protecting the Colorado River corridor.

Impressed panelists encouraged the Glenwood students to apply for grant funds to implement their ideas. They did, and became the first team of high school students in their state to obtain a Greater Outdoor Colorado Grant. The city matched the state's funding and students ultimately received $66,000 to plan and develop a riverside pocket park. (Lieberman and Hoody, 1998)

The students' articulate speaking skills, developed in part through participating in an EIC program, won them the respect of the city's leaders. And the challenge of writing a grant application was a real-world test of their writing skills. The SEER study is demonstrating that using the environment as an integrating context can improve test scores, enhance citizenship, *and* improve the quality of the local environment.

Environment-Based Education: Creating High Performance Schools and Students

A study published in September 2000, commissioned by the National Environmental Education and Training Foundation (NEETF), echoes many of the findings of the SEER study. The study

focused on five schools in Texas, North Carolina, and Wisconsin, a
model school program involving five schools in Florida, and a
statewide program in Kentucky. The schools had all chosen place-
based education as a core instructional strategy. Many were in urban
neighborhoods with diverse racial profiles and high percentages of
students receiving free or reduced-price lunches. The introduction to
the study says:

> *Since 1983, with the release of* A Nation at Risk, *Americans have
> been engaged in a journey toward creating more effective schools.... The
> school reform movement is calling for well-educated individuals who have a
> deep and abiding knowledge of the world in which they live. Society is ask-
> ing for citizens who are prepared to take active roles in their communities.
> Business is calling for "renaissance workers," workers skilled in the leadership
> competencies that will be required in the increasingly complex global environ-
> ment....* Environment-based education is a maturing discipline well
> suited to achieving these goals. *[Author's emphasis] (Glenn, 2000)*

Standardized testing of students in the schools studied showed that:

- Reading scores improved, sometimes spectacularly.
- Math scores also improved.
- Students performed better in science and social studies.
- Students developed the ability to make connections and trans-
  fer their knowledge from familiar to unfamiliar contexts.
- Students learned to "do science" rather than just learn about
  science.
- Classroom discipline problems declined.
- Every student had the opportunity to learn at a higher level.
  (Numerous teachers in Kentucky indicated that students pre-
  viously performing at low academic levels "came alive" when
  introduced to an environment-based curriculum.)

The Isaac Dickson Elementary School in Asheville, North
Carolina, is a K–5 school in which 50 percent of the students come
from low-income families. "Academic progress for our students is
increasingly more challenging," says Principal Vicki Deneen, "because
of the poverty issues that consume families living in the projects."
Environmental education with a service-learning focus was imple-

mented to help students meet the state learning standards. Teachers, students, community members, government agencies, and community organizations collaborated on three schoolwide learning projects—a gardening and science club, the MAGIC program (Mountain Area Gardens in Community), which involved school and community gardening and food preparation, and the re-establishment of a school-yard nature trail.

The results? "During the 1998–99 school year, students at Isaac Dickson Elementary improved their reading, math and writing skills as measured on state achievement tests. Overall, school achievement was exemplary, with actual growth 9.1 points above expected growth."

Let's look a little more closely at the math scores. From 1998 to 1999, the statewide math scores for fourth graders showed an increase of 15 percent in students scoring at the "proficient" level. The percentage of fourth graders at Dickson performing at the proficient level increased by 31 percent. Fifth graders statewide showed an increase of 3 percent while those at Dickson showed an increase of 14 percent and went from scoring slightly below the state average to well above. The study finds similar results in reading and math scores at the Hawley Environmental Elementary School in Milwaukee, Wisconsin—a school surrounded by city streets, with an asphalt play-ground and a student population of which 71 percent receive free or reduced-price lunch.

How about science and social studies? The Tompkinsville Elementary School in Tompkinsville, Kentucky, serves 630 rural students, also with a high percentage of students qualifying for the lunch program. Prior to 1995, science, reading, and social studies scores on the Kentucky Instructional Results Information System (KIRIS) assessment were low. Then, Tompkinsville got an outdoor classroom. A group of teachers and community members built trails, observation decks, and an outdoor amphitheater; they also planted a garden. Concurrently, the teachers turned the curriculum out into the community. Principal Cecelia Stevens comments, "Our students might explore how logging affects the economy, look at the pros and cons, and visit local lumber mills." Since 1995, the scores on the KIRIS assessment have risen consistently, with an increase of 25 percent in science scores and 40 percent in social studies scores over four years. A more recent study, published in *Forum*, a publication of the Funder's Forum on Environment and Education, recounts the test scores for eighth graders on the Oregon Assessment Test from the Environmental Middle School (EMS) in Portland, Oregon. Over the past five years, teachers at this urban school have developed a curriculum built around rivers, mountains, and forests." Tuesdays and Thursdays at EMS are dedicated to field studies restoration work and community service. Students plant native species, serve meals to the homeless, and sample the Willamette River, developing an exceptional knowledge of and attachment to their home. " (Smith, 2001)

The percentage of EMS eighth graders meeting or exceeding state standards in reading/literature, mathematics, writing, and math problem solving has risen substantially above the state average in the past three years. One interesting statistic: Ninety-six percent of EMS eighth graders meet or exceed state standards for math problem solving, compared to only 65 percent of eighth graders at comparable middle schools.

The same kind of story appears to be emerging in Louisiana bayou country, about 30 miles northeast of Baton Rouge. East Feliciana Parish faces numerous challenges: "low income populations with a limited tax base, struggling resource-based economies, a shortage of certified teachers, a large proportion of students considered 'at risk' and few career opportunities for high school graduates hoping to stay in the area." (Null, 2002)

Concerned by low science test scores on state assessments and a lack of science background among teachers, superintendent Daisy Slan decided to try something new. Book learning and rote memorization weren't working, so with support from the Delta Rural Systemic Initiative of the National Science Foundation and the Rural School and Community Trust, the district implemented Project Connect, a math and science professional development program with an emphasis on place-based education. In just the second full year of the program, students' performance on the Louisiana Educational Assessment Program (LEAP) improved significantly. "Although fourth grade students in East Feliciana's three elementary schools (Clinton, Jackson and Slaughter) continued to rank below the overall state average in their scores taken as a whole, the number of students passing the science portion increased thirteen percent." (Null, 2002) In response to these hopeful indicators, superintendent Slan is planning to expand place-based approaches across the curriculum.

Another measure of achievement is college acceptance rates. The

Llano Grande Center at Edcouch-Elsa High School in southernmost Texas has been a Rural School and Community Trust site for almost a decade. In the tiny, mostly Hispanic towns in this area, 90 percent of the households have incomes of less than $10,000 and 91 percent of parents lack a high school diploma. "Yet in the last decade, Edcouch-Elsa High School has sent 45 students to elite colleges and universities such as Stanford, Brown, Yale and Princeton while 65 percent go on to some form of higher education—well above national norms for Hispanic students." (Zibart, 2002)

This litany of results may still not allay one of the concerns lurking in many readers' minds: "Well great, they perform well on tests, but can they *think?*" The Environmental Middle School results from Oregon suggest an answer, and the final case study of the NEETF study supports it. The case study was conducted at Condit Elementary School in Houston, Texas, by researcher Carol Basile. The school population comes from both sides of the tracks, according to Basile, and includes a representative mix of Hispanic, African American, Caucasian, and Asian students. The school is considered a high-achieving school with strong parental and administrative support. Basile's study was about as controlled as you can get for this kind of educational research. She split a group of 45 third graders into two groups and taught one group traditionally and the other group using an environment-based approach. Her objective was to determine if the third graders could transfer their learning from the content covered to other contexts.

The traditional group experienced classroom-based instruction (with the exception of one weekly nature walk and one field trip to a local nature center) to learn about habitat. The children read and discussed forest, prairie, wetland, and urban habitats. They learned about habitats through art projects, worksheets, and environmental activities that could be done in the classroom. None of the activities required any kind of systematic investigative process.

The experimental group used Nature at Your Doorstep, a skill-based curriculum based in the scientific method. In each investigation, students "became scientists" by reading about and researching topics such as habitat, biodiversity, trees, or food webs. They developed their own questions and collected their own data. They learned to analyze data by charting and graphing. Every week the students explored a new problem, i.e., they might try to find out whether trees can be habitats for some animal. Students worked outdoors three out of five days, and took one field trip to the local nature center. (Glenn, 2000)

Using a wide array of indicators, Basile found that while both groups were able to transfer their knowledge from the learning situation to a similar situation (referred to as *near transfer*), only the environment-based group of third graders could transfer their learning to a vastly different context (*far transfer*). In other words, the students hadn't just consumed a set of facts; they had developed a set of higher-order cognitive skills in observation, analysis, and problem solving that they could carry with them as tools to use in other settings.

Of course, we want our students to test well, but what we want even more are students who, when they get dropped into new situations, can figure out how to approach a problem. We want them to ask: What resources are available, what do I already know, how can I get started, and who can I get to help me solve this? Both the SEER and NEETF studies suggest that community-based and place-based education successfully increase academic achievement *and* give students the skills to solve problems.

Place-Based Education and the Cultivation of Stewardship

All of the above sounds reasonably persuasive—unless you don't really think that academic performance is the true measure of program success. I was first exposed to this perspective in the course of a discussion about place-based education programs with Ted Smith, director of the Kendall Foundation in Boston, a well-known leader in environmental funding. When we talked about academic achievement, Ted kind of grimaced. "Well, test scores are all fine and good," he acknowledged, "but what I really want to know is if these programs help kids become better stewards of the land and water. Does place-based education actually change their environmental behavior?"

The answer to this question is still forming. When you ask this question of academics, researchers, and program developers, the generic response is, "Well, anecdotally we've got lots of studies that suggest significant change, but there are really not a lot of hard numbers." The recently formed Place-based Education Evaluation

Collaborative (PEEC) is conducting research to generate these hard numbers. This collaboration between a number of northern New England place-based education programs and the Upper Valley Community Foundation is interested in documenting changes in environmental attitudes and behaviors, but it will be a few years before definitive results are available.

Nonetheless, let me share with you just a few of the existing research studies that take a stab at quantifying the relationship between place-based education and changes in environmental attitudes and behavior. In a study entitled *Schoolyard Learning: The Impact of Schoolgrounds*, researchers at the Education Development Center in Newton, Massachusetts, pulled together the available studies that look at how schoolyards shape environmental attitudes. (Education Development Center, 2000) This study was commissioned by the Boston Schoolyards Initiative because their funders want to know if pulling up all that asphalt and creating naturalized playgrounds throughout the city really makes any difference. There's some evidence to support revving up the jackhammers. These results are relevant not only for the Boston Schoolyards Initiative, but also for place-based educators because many school improvement projects include transforming the schoolyard into a more suitable learning environment for teachers and students.

In 1989, Margarette Harvey studied 850 elementary students from 21 schools in the south of England. The schools she chose represented a range of types of schoolyards—from undifferentiated pavement to completely naturalized yards with ponds, trees, hideouts, and gardens. As you would expect, the children from naturalized schoolyards had more botanical knowledge. And there was a direct correlation between the scope of the children's knowledge and the amount of vegetation and complexity of landscape features. But there's more: "When compared to their peers from schools with undeveloped school grounds, students who had been exposed to more vegetation and landscape features showed higher scores for pastoralism (the enjoyment of the natural environment in an intellectual fashion) and lower scores for human dominance (the belief in humans' rights to use technology to adapt to and dominate nature.)" (Education Development Center, 2000) What Harvey is saying is that as the diversity of the natural landscape on schoolyards increases, there's an increase in children's appreciation of experiences in the natural world. These changes in environmental attitudes provide the affective basis for stewardship behavior—for acting in ways that improve the quality of the environment.

A study in Texas entitled *The Effect of an Interdisciplinary Garden Program on the Environmental Attitudes of Elementary School Students* supports Harvey's findings. (Education Development Center, 2000) Using the same pastoralism and human dominance instruments, they found that children who participated in a school gardening program showed more positive environmental attitudes than peers who did not participate.

Then what about behavior? Lynnette Zelezny combed the research journals and found all the studies from 1974 to 1999 that examined the effects of different kinds of environmental education programs on changes in environmental behavior. (Zelezny, 1999) The programs studied ranged from nature camps and residential environmental programs to short- and long-term school-based programs. Thus one of her topics of interest was the effectiveness of nature programs at environmental centers versus school-based programs that involved nature studies in the local landscape and community. The following summarizes her main findings:

a. **"Educational interventions that actively involved participants were more effective in improving environmental behavior than those that did not."** This is kind of a no-brainer, but it's nice to see it confirmed by research. It echoes the Texas study of third graders showing that when the same content was presented to two groups, students who actually engaged in investigations developed sturdier skills.

b. **"Intervention effectiveness was greater among participants who were 18 years old or younger."** Another no-brainer supporting the get-them-while-they're-young attitude. Forget about those college students if you want real change.

c. **"Classroom interventions improved environmental behavior more effectively than interventions in non-traditional settings."** Though the first two points are kind of obvious, this last one is significant. In other words, in-depth school-based programs are more likely to change behavior than programs at the environment camp that are not integrated into the curriculum. For instance, this suggests that an on-going study of the vernal pool adjacent to the schoolyard is going to have more of an effect on students' environmental behaviors than a week-long stay at a nature camp. For funders trying to figure out how to get the most bang for their buck, this is a significant finding. And it provides some solid footing for those educators trying to weave environmental education into the fabric of public schools. If we can believe this study, then school-based programs do have the potential for creating persistent environmental stewardship behavior.

Let me end with a recent research study that suggests a whole other domain we should be considering. In Denmark and Sweden in recent years there's a new kind of preschool program roughly translated as Outdoors in all Weather. (Grahn et al., 1997) The core idea is to spend the majority of time, say 60 to 80 percent of the school day, in the out-of-doors. Doesn't matter whether it's sunny and beautiful or foggy and dreary or windy and snowy, put on those wellies and out we go. There are programs in rural villages as well as in Copenhagen and Stockholm, so four-year-olds may be gardening and fishing, or they may be exploring alleyways and feeding pigeons. What's the result? Students in the Outdoors in all Weather programs are suffering from 80 percent fewer infectious diseases (colds, ear infections, sore throats, whooping cough) than children in conventional indoor programs. That's huge! Can you think of a better reason for doing place-based education than to keep your children healthier? It makes sense, of course, since putting children in close proximity to each other in containers of poorly circulated air guarantees more effective transmission of viruses and bacteria. And it does, perhaps, correlate with the SEER findings of lower absenteeism in EIC programs. So here's another charge for you place-based educators: Start collecting data on nurse and doctor visits for children in your programs compared to children who aren't getting out as much. This kind of data *will* have an impact on parents!

David Sobel

Building a Three-Legged Stool of Academic Achievement, Social Capital, and Environmental Quality

The Place-based Education Evaluation Collaborative has many partners in their efforts: the CO-SEED program of Antioch New England Graduate School in Keene, NH, the Sustainable Schools and the Forest for Every Classroom programs at Shelburne Farms near Burlington, Vermont, the Community Mapping project of the Orton Family Foundation and the Vermont Institute of Natural Science in Woodstock, Vermont, and the Wellborn Ecology Fund in Hanover, New Hampshire. The Collaborative and its partners' aspirations are broader than just looking at academic achievement. While we all started out thinking that our focus was on school improvement and academic achievement, we have come to realize that our focus is equally on creating vital communities and preserving the quality of the environment. We are now aware that there is a dynamic tension between these three elements—that together they form a three-legged stool that will not stand if any one of the legs is missing. Try to improve a school without actively engaging the community, and your efforts won't garner the budget support and human capital necessary for success. Emphasize community development without the involvement of the school and you won't have the youthful energy that makes projects work. Build thriving local economies with little concern for the environment and you'll find that businesses will have trouble attracting workers because people aren't willing to raise children amidst deteriorated air and water.

Past Rural School and Community Trust director Paul Nachtigal clarified the necessity of this kind of systems thinking.

When schools focus only on how education benefits the individual, they become the enemy of the community. They educate young people to leave and so fulfill the prophecy that these places are doomed to poverty, decline and despair. Instead, we intend to rally communities to reinvent their schools as engines of renewal for the public good. (Cushman, 1997)

Creating Social Capital

Social capital is Harvard sociologist Robert Putnam's term for the willingness and capacity of individuals to work for the collective good of a community. When lots of people are willing and able to

While we all started out thinking that our focus was on school improvement and academic achievement, we have come to realize that our focus is equally on creating vital communities and preserving the quality of the environment.

run for town office or serve on civic committees, that's an indicator of high social capital. Or when it's easy to find moms and dads who want to coach the soccer teams in the town recreational league or lots of people show up for the annual roadside trash removal—yup, high social capital. Increased social capital leads to a greater sense of personal well-being amongst citizens, which ultimately translates into economic well-being for their communities.

For instance, in 1997, students in Cedar Bluff, Alabama, launched a computer assembly and software development business that takes orders from the public and serves a network of rural schools. It went on to win a grant to connect the entire county's school system. While the students get technological and business experience, the community gets better computer services and significant cost savings. In addition, students recognize that perhaps they don't have to migrate to Birmingham or Huntsville to find challenging jobs. The wealth of the students' intelligence stays in the community.

In Guilford, Vermont, the middle school students write and publish the community newspaper—not the traditional school newspaper, but the actual town publication, with accident reports, selectmen's meeting results, notices of community events, and features on town residents. Seventh and eighth graders serve as reporters, copy editors, advertising salespeople, and designers. Working on the paper helps students meet Vermont State Curriculum Standards and provides the town with a valuable communication resource. Community members frequently comment on how much more connected they feel to their neighbors and town affairs as a result of the student-produced publication.

Julie Bartsch's recent book, *Community Lessons: Integrating Service Learning into K-12 Curriculum*, is a brilliant compendium of many of these kinds of projects in Massachusetts. In each case she articulates both the academic gains for the students and the societal gains for the community. In one of my favorite examples, she describes the need that stimulated a project in the mill city of North Adams.

> *In order to remain fiscally solvent, the North Adams Regional Hospital made necessary but drastic changes in the way it conducted business. In the process, the pediatric wing closed and many children had to use the emergency room as their primary care facility. Children expressed fear and discomfort about their experiences at the hospital.*

Recognizing that the children's anxiety constituted a community need, one kindergarten teacher, Roberta Sullivan, worked with her students to change the climate of the emergency room.

> *After touring the facility with their teacher, these children created artwork to decorate the walls and purchased toys for the waiting room area. More importantly, the class wrote a book to be read by the parent and child while sitting in the waiting room. Interviewing hospital personnel, from the CEO to members of the housekeeping staff, the children not only collected*

pertinent information to include in their book, but also made discoveries of their own regarding medical careers, safety precautions and germs.

This was valuable learning for the children, but an immeasurable benefit to the community as well. Bartsch's description of the "societal gains" for this project illustrates the broader impact.

As a result of the kindergartners' taking the time to collaborate on ways to improve the new pediatric emergency room setting, many ill children now have positive experiences at the hospital. The staff at the hospital wrote the children a note after the redecorated emergency room had been in use for some time. The note explained that the hospital routinely had to use a restraining board with uncooperative children. The note went on to say that since the students had done their work in the hospital, this board had not been needed. The doctors and nurses credited the students with this success. (Bartsch, 2001)

This example also reminds me of a conversation I had with a well-known teacher educator many years ago. "I can tell I'm in the presence of a good teacher," she said, "when I walk into the classroom and see something I've never seen before." In this case, Roberta Sullivan turned a need into an opportunity and created a one-of-a-kind curriculum project with integrated academic and community benefits.

Our hope is that these kinds of projects will inspire local citizens to take a more active role in the schools and community and that students come to think of community service the way they think about going to the movies—it's a normal thing you do every week or so. Though social capital research is in its infancy, there's lots of qualitative evidence that indicates we're heading in the right direction. For instance, in East Feliciana Parish, after a science improvement project increased student test scores, parent participation in school-sponsored activities went on the upswing, as did more widespread community involvement (Null, 2002). On a recent Martin Luther King Day, 60 volunteers, including parents, teachers, office staff, a custodian, a school board member, and the superintendent, constructed nature trails at all three district elementary schools.

One of the goals for place-based educators over the next five years is to start to quantify the impact of place-based education on social capital and community vitality, as measured by sustainable economic development. We think we'll find something analogous to the relationship between consumer confidence and the health of the economy. As the quality of schooling improves, the willingness to contribute to the community and the resulting satisfaction with the communal quality of life will increase as well.

Preserving Environmental Quality

Educators are hoping to begin quantifying the impacts of place-based education on environmental quality: 15,429 tons of paper and cans recycled, 60,000 acres of rainforest protected, 3,415 natural areas made accessible to the public, 527 cases of water pollution detected and remediated. Regrettably, these are all fabricated numbers. But wouldn't it be impressive if we were able to collect this kind of data? We could then figure out the cost per unit of preservation—the cost to protect an acre of rainforest, or the cost per ton of paper recycled. The economists would have a field day!

Some schools are beginning to collect this data and use it to lobby for constructive change in their schools and community. This year the students in the Advanced Placement environmental science class at Peoples Academy (the public high school) in Morrisville, Vermont, conducted research locally on air quality, the impact of phosphates on algae growth in lakes, different techniques for managing purple loosestrife, and waste reduction in the school. The waste-reduction project is a masterpiece of data collection and analysis that resulted in specific cost-saving recommendations for the school. (Peoples Academy students, 2001) First, the students quantified the amount of solid waste generated in the cafeteria—14,866 pounds per year. Next, they determined what percentage of that could be recycled or composted—80 percent. Then they calculated the cost of new equipment and changed procedures in the school (for instance, if styrofoam trays and plates were abandoned and dishwashers had to be used to wash trays and plates, there would be an increased cost for labor, soap, and hot water). When all was said and done, their report contended that the school could save $5,736 a year by implementing a comprehensive program to reduce solid waste. Great math and science went into this project, and resulted in a significant potential savings for the community.

Drop by drop, teachers and students are making a substantial contribution to environmental monitoring, species protection, land preservation, and air quality improvement in place-based education projects. The following is a kind of master list that suggests some of the domains in which gains are being made, with an illustrative example of each:

Water quality monitoring. Students at Taylor County High School in Perry, Florida, are responsible for monitoring the Econfina River and have now been contracted by Buckeye Cellulose to help in the restoration of San Pedro Bay.

School recycling. Students at the Wheelock Elementary School in Keene, New Hampshire, recently began composting post-consumer food waste from the school lunch program. The composted waste will be used in the school gardens and distributed free of charge to gardeners in the neighborhood adjacent to the school.

Schoolyard naturalization. The Evergreen Foundation of Toronto and Vancouver has helped more than one thousand Canadian schools transform their schoolyards into green spaces filled with native flora. (Here's a study unto itself: How much biodiversity has been reintroduced into different regions as a function of naturalized schoolyards?)

Habitat restoration. The STRAW Program (Students and Teachers Restoring a Watershed) works with more than 50 schools in the San Francisco Bay area on restoring riparian habitat, clearing debris from streams, and researching native species.

Natural areas interpretation. The third graders in Wendy Oellers's class at the Gilford Elementary School in Gilford, New Hampshire, have recently completed a nature trail map and guide for the conservation land adjacent to the school. This guide complements a beautifully crafted display board of the trail created by an Eagle Scout student from the high school.

Aquaponics and waste management. High school students in Dumas, Texas, combined fish farming and hydroponics (growing plants without soil) in a project to recycle biological wastes from a pig farm.

Toxins reduction. Students in Floral Park, New York, researched and analyzed different solvents based on cost, environmental impact, and cleaning effectiveness, in order to make recommendations for reducing toxins in the classrooms.

Energy conservation. The Green Schools program of the Alliance to Save Energy works with schools across the country to monitor and analyze energy- consumption patterns and then propose a plan for energy reduction. Some of the money saved is used to create other conservation initiatives.

Green buildings. Students at the Yampa Mountain High School in Glenwood Springs, Colorado, designed and built a solar-powered, energy-efficient science lab using strawbale building techniques.

Invasive species control. The Illinois-Indiana Sea Grant program trains 4-H leaders and teachers to engage their students in controlling the spread of purple loosestrife, an invasive wetlands plant.

And this just scratches the surface. Schools can be the epicenter for environmental change in their communities, motivating civic officials to take action. It's hard, after all, to say no to your own children. And there's no dearth of problems to take on. Just the other day with students from the Beebe School in Malden, Massachusetts, the teachers were wondering about getting middle school students involved in Canada goose waste-abatement techniques at Fellsmere Pond. (That's a polite way of saying, how do we deal with the water pollution caused by so much goose poop?) Please contact us if you have any ideas!

Sowing Seeds

So maybe you've heard enough to know that place-based education is your cup of tea and you're convinced it really does make a difference for children, communities, and the environment. The problem is, you're thinking, it sounds great in all those other places, but it'll never work in my neighborhood. The streets are too dangerous, the principal's about to retire and doesn't want to start anything new, the teachers are stressed out by the state testing requirements. Not to worry. It's your turn to become one of those oozing drops of water. Read on and I'll show you the crannies you can slip into to start your work.

The CO-SEED Project (Community-based School Environmental Education) is a regional place-based education initiative I've been involved in for the last six years. Since CO-SEED is in my neighborhood, I'm going to use it as my touchstone for the narrative that follows, to provide illustrations, structural examples, and a departure point from which to go out and explore other initiatives. What will emerge is set of guidelines and strategies that will help you get things percolating in your community.

CO-SEED first sprouted in 1997 at the Great Brook Middle School in Antrim, New Hampshire, and has since spread to seven school districts covering more than a dozen communities in Vermont, New Hampshire, and Massachusetts. The project staff also administers the Green Schools grant programs which provides support for school/community environmentalism in classrooms, schools, and urban and rural neighborhoods throughout the country. Keep in mind that my goal is not to advocate for one particular model, but rather to provide the ethnographic particularities that illustrate how the process has worked in a variety of places.

Many of these large bioregional projects are supported with foundation funds and federal grants. It costs money to create demonstration projects, conduct evaluations, and document and publicize the results. On the other hand, there are innumerable examples of small, emergent place-based projects that cost little or nothing and are helping to change schools. Through our Green Schools grant program, we've provided more than two hundred small grants (of about $2,000 each) to help schools naturalize schoolyards, stock streams with trout, study squirrels, and create environmental art. It doesn't cost much to get the ball rolling, and once it's rolling, it gathers momentum and can often generate its own funding.

The Master Plan

CO-SEED is a partnership of school districts, community organizations, environmental learning centers (ELCs), and a higher education institution—in this case, Antioch New England Graduate School. Through a community vision-to-action forum and a number of other outreach mechanisms, we collaborate with the superintendent's office, the mayor's office, the historical society, the public works department, parent groups, and a brownfields redevelopment organization. In Littleton, New Hampshire, for example, community partners include the town planner's office, the town engineer, local businesses, the historical society, the solid waste manager, and a local group called Envisioning Littleton's Future.

In each setting we:

- Work with a SEED team, a steering committee composed of teachers, administrators, community members, town officials, and sometimes students. The SEED team directs the project and distributes small grants to teachers in the district schools who want to conduct place-based education projects.
- Provide funding and guidance for a half-time environmental educator from a local environmental learning center to work in the school.
- Provide on-going professional development in place-based education for teachers and community members.
- Conduct community vision-to-action forums and other engagement activities to weave together community and school action plans for local improvement.

The Seeds of CO-SEED

But how did we get to this point? It's always fun to tease out the genealogy of a project or an idea—like asking your parents how they first met, or encouraging a musician to reveal where the melody for that hit song came from. My own first memories go back almost a decade before the project started to my own real life problem-solving challenge in Antrim, New Hampshire. Antrim, a blue-collar, slightly run-down mill town, was a place I passed through once in a while on my way to somewhere else. But this town proved to be a rich learning ground for me, and my students, one fall. For the Environmental Interpretation course I was teaching that semester, I wanted to get away from the "this-is-a-red-maple, this-boulder-is-a-remnant-of-the-last-glacier" approach to interpretation. So I structured the course around a real problem: The Society for the Protection of New Hampshire Forests needed a trail guide for a piece of land they owned in Antrim. Our job was to do a resource inventory, interview local residents, map a potential trail, and draft a trail guide. I wanted the students to use local stories to disclose the unique cultural and natural history of this edge-of-town farm that stretched from Main Street down to the floodplain forest along the Contoocook River. The final product would have a real audience of community members rather than just me as their professor. And so, we began to interview community elders who could tell us how this place had shaped their lives.

Dorothy McCabe, thin, strong, and as well preserved as a cedar post, captivated us with her stories as we sat in the parlor of her old home in what had just become the Forest Society's McCabe Forest Preserve.

I remember when I was a girl and it was a hot May afternoon. We all had a favorite swimming place down by a bend in the river—near the old oxbow. It was sandy there and deep enough to dive into. When I got there I noticed three big funny-looking water bugs perched on the water. I was going to investigate, but the black flies were so bad, I decided just to strip down and jump in the water. Well, as soon as I jumped in the river, I was scared by the ferociously churning water—like the Loch Ness monster was coming to the surface. And then three deer charge out of the water and stampede into the woods. Turns out those three water bugs had been their noses and the deer had been suspended in the water, just their noses sticking up so they could breath. This is how they got a bit of respite from the black flies. (Sobel, 1999)

Other community members recalled how in winter, in the days when all the fields were cut for hay, you could start up on Elm Street, cross Main Street (someone had to make sure no cars were coming), and sled clear down, past the mowing, almost all the way to the river. Others recalled skating on the pond that had filled the pit excavated to provide clay for the brickyard. "Antrim children used to ramble and explore all over McCabe Forest," I thought as we were wrapping up the project that winter. "Isn't it strange that we haven't seen a local kid here all fall? And aren't those remembered activities the basis of good education and a solid connection with the community?"

Susie Denehy, education director at the Harris Center for Conservation Education in adjacent Hancock, had a related thought when she started working with students at the Great Brook Middle School around 1995. One of the core books for fifth graders in her district is *My Side of the Mountain* by Jean Craighead George. In the book, twelve-year-old Sam Gribley leaves the city to spend the winter in the woods on his grandfather's land in the Catskills. He learns to live off the land using only the bare essentials, and he builds an awesome shelter. The Great Brook teachers brought the book alive by taking a field trip to the Harris Center where the students could build their own shelters. But when Susie arrived on the scene, she was puzzled. "Why are we carting students in buses all the way from Antrim to Hancock when the McCabe Forest is only a ten-minute walk from the school? If we do this activity in their town, it will encourage students to use the forest for exploration and adventures." From this seed of an idea grew a symbiotic relationship between the school and local resources.

Great Brook fifth grade teachers Ann Kenney and Barbara Black recognized that using the local environment as a teaching tool held lots of promise for enriching the curriculum and motivating students. With help from the Harris Center and Antioch New England, they developed the Wetlands Project to take advantage of the namesake Great Brook, which ran behind the middle school. Over the course of three years, a boardwalk and elegant gateway were designed and built by students working with community artisans-in-residence, a theater piece was produced, and a comprehensive fifth grade water-studies curriculum emerged. Once the students understood how to use the pH monitors and test the water of the marshland behind the school, they were able to expand outward to other places in the watershed.

"We wanted the students to look at a stream environment that was different from the marsh behind the school," recalls Ann Kenney. "No Name Brook [a stretch of Great Brook that flows through McCabe] is steep and rocky and we thought the water quality and macroinvertebrates might be different, so we started making regular field trips to McCabe to expand our water studies curriculum."

Indeed, water testing in No Name Brook helped the students understand that once you've seen one stream, you haven't seen them

"Why are we carting students in buses all the way from Antrim to Hancock when the McCabe Forest is only a ten-minute walk from the school? If we do this activity in their town, it will encourage students to use the forest for exploration and adventures."

all. And the teachers' eyes started to open as well. Why stop at shelter building and stream studies? How else could the community and local places be used to enliven the curriculum?

Establishing Roots

At Antioch New England, we were ready to take the next step. Our Wetlands Project had helped to spawn the Harris Center/Great Brook collaboration. The Rachel Marshall Outdoor Learning Laboratory in Keene was successfully engaging teachers, students, and community members in designing a citywide learning laboratory. And yet another effort, the Valley Quest project of Antioch's Vital Communities of the Upper Valley Initiative, was helping teachers create treasure hunts to the distinctive natural and cultural landmarks in Connecticut River towns in New Hampshire and Vermont. The common theme in these efforts was our desire to bring the environment and the community into the core of the curriculum. For too long, we felt, environmental education had been like art class. It happened for 50 minutes a week when the naturalist brought the owl into the classroom and the teacher got a break. It was a tassel on the edge of the fabric, not the warp. We thought, let's find some schools who want to make ecological literacy a serious part of the school philosophy. Let's find schools that want to ground their curriculum in their local places—the natural environment and the social institutions of the town.

And so CO-SEED was born in 1997. We approached the Harris Center, the Great Brook Middle School, and the Antrim community first to see if they wanted to collectively pilot the project. Within the following year we created similar partnerships in different geographic regions and with different environmental partners. In the upper Connecticut River valley, in conjunction with Hulbert Outdoor Center, we partnered with the new Rivendell Interstate School District stretching from Vershire, Vermont, across the river to Orford, New Hampshire. In the forest-products industry world north of the White Mountain notches, we joined forces with the communities of Gorham, Randolph, and Shelburne, New Hampshire, and with two environmental organizations, Trail Master and the Appalachian Mountain Club (AMC). In 2000–2001, we developed similar partnerships in Littleton and Gilford, New Hampshire, adding the New Hampshire Audubon Society to the mix. And to test our model in an urban site, we developed a partnership between the Beebe School and the Stone Zoo in Malden, Massachusetts, a city of approximately fifty-six thousand located just north of Boston, with an ethnically diverse student population.

Though each of the sites has its own unique characteristics and has developed in its own way, we have chosen these sites on the basis of shared preconditions. The core principles for how to move forward with our brand of school reform, community development, and environmental resource protection are consistent across sites as well.

Though I'll be describing CO-SEED operations below, you'll find a co-evolution of similar strategies in community and place-based projects around the country.

Notes on Soil Preparation

One of the CO-SEED mantras that we continually recite to ourselves is "Depth over Breadth." As we're encouraging teachers to do fewer things in greater depth, and encouraging environmental centers to offer fewer owl programs and develop more solid relationships with schools, we are also challenging ourselves to commit a substantial chunk of our energy to only a few school districts. Change only happens when you dig in, or, to maintain the droplet metaphor, soak in. Since we can only work deeply with a few schools and communities, we prospect for ones that really *want* to change, as intently as if we were looking for vein of precious ore. We take core samples and evaluate how much raw material there is to work with. It's like the old light bulb joke:

> *Question: "How many psychotherapists does it take to change a lightbulb?"*
> *Answer: "Only one. But the light bulb has to really want to be changed."*

For educators, administrators, community activists, and environmental educators wishing to initiate small-scale place-based education projects, I've created a set of guidelines for how to do your own prospecting.

Guidelines for Identifying Good Places to Start

There are signs of a predisposition toward place-based education. We often say, "Don't throw seed on untilled soil." When we were contacted by Robin Jorgensen, magnet theme coordinator at the Beebe Environmental and Health Sciences School, she explained, "We're an environmental magnet school in name, but not in practice, and we'd like you to help us with the practice." The existence of the magnet theme and a staff person dedicated to making the theme happen indicated to us that a predisposition was there—the soil was ready for sowing.

Hint: Look for the presence of active community groups seeking greater student involvement, such as a recreation department that needs more activity leaders for afterschool programs. Or listen for rumblings in the school or in the parent-teacher group about the need to raise test scores or reduce youth violence. Place-based education can be a ready solution for a variety of school and community problems.

Administrative support is strong. Place-based education will go nowhere fast without leadership near or at the top of the school or the district. When we realized that Sandy McGonagle, the assistant principal in Gilford who was enthusiastic about CO-SEED, was also an active member of the conservation commission, we knew this was a good sign.

Hint: Identify administrators who belong to the local historical society or the state Audubon organization, participate in a community-supported agriculture project, or are faculty sponsors for the school newspaper or the outing club. Administrators who play an active role in nonschool organizations have the values and energy to expand the scope of the school's reach. Other words we live by: "If you want to get something done, ask a busy person." Also, it's worthwhile to either find supportive school board members or become one yourself.

A cadre of committed teachers exists. You don't need many, but you need a dedicated handful. We started our program at Great Brook School in Antrim because two fifth grade teachers and the Extended Learning Program teacher had already implemented the Wetlands Project. There need to be teachers who will quickly pick up the ball and run with it.

Hint: Are there teachers who are already active grantwriters, or who already take students out into the community to do curriculum projects? Or are there professionals in the community who used to be teachers? In Antrim, one of our strongest community allies was the mailman, Rob Zwirner, who used to teach at a Quaker high school. Also active on the conservation commission, he became a dependable field-trip leader.

Active dialogue exists between school and community. We were attracted to Littleton, New Hampshire, because community members had spent 18 months with an architectural consulting firm in a design process called Envisioning Littleton's Future. A *USA Today* article commented, "The town and school boards realized that their futures are intertwined: Without more resources in the schools, Littleton could not develop a strong labor force and attract investments." (El Nasser, 2000) When the community took the next step and decided to merge the town and school district budgeting procedures, we knew we were in the right place.

Hint: School projects that aim to save the town or city some money are great motivators for getting community leaders interested in collaboration. Initiate projects that target solid-waste reduction or energy savings for the school. Get a teacher interested in trying to decrease vandalism in the town park. Another strategy is to recruit recently hired or appointed town employees onto your team. In Gilford, New Hampshire, a new town planner was hired soon after the CO-SEED project got going. He saw the community engagement activities as a great way to meet members of the community and establish his credibility.

An environmental learning center (ELC) is ready and willing to join forces. CO-SEED strives to help environmental organizations become more effective. To do so, ELCs must move beyond the short-term programs to establish in-depth relationships with a school district. In the Lakes Region of New Hampshire, Prescott Farm Audubon staff were excited about the opportunity to work with local schools because they saw it as a way to establish a broader constituency for their relatively new site in the region.

Hint: Be broad-minded about potential environmental partners. In Keene, New Hampshire, one of our primary partners has been the city recreation department. One of our recent Green Schools grants went to a teacher who is going to work with the local snowmobiling club to map winter trails. In Colorado, one of the community mapping projects mapped accident sites for the local ambulance service. At CO-SEED we call it the Strange Bedfellows Principle—sometimes the most interesting projects emerge out of partnerships between organizations that are seemingly antithetical.

If you're trying to start a large regional program, our sense is, wait to go forward until all of the above conditions exist. Whereas in the beginning we courted our first three sets of schools and communities, for subsequent schools and communities we initiated an application and interview process. Schools need to prove to us that they're ready. We've also implemented contractual relationships with schools so they know what they're getting from us and what we expect from them. And from the beginning we make a commitment to develop a long-term plan to help them sustain the changes that will ensue. We're planting perennials, not annuals.

For schools and communities just getting started, use any of the hints as starting points, and remember that it's okay to start small. A one-week program this year can turn into a month-long program next year. One Eagle Scout's project for a badge can turn into a service learning program for the high school biology class in the future. Small grants, which are easier to obtain, will get you launched more quickly so you can galvanize the attention and support needed to expand in the future. Remember, getting started is half of the battle.

Creating Place-Based Schools: Core Strategies

You've got your foot in the door, the principal likes your idea, and the owner of the local supermarket wants to carry produce from the school garden. What are the next steps? Let me provide you with two guiding principles and then elaborate on six strategies for implementing place-based education.

To illustrate the two principles, I'd like to introduce two significant players in the work we've been doing. The first is Haven Neal, a retired paper company employee and town forester for Gorham, New Hampshire. When we were exploring the idea of starting a CO-SEED project in Gorham, Haven was skeptical. But as he listened and got involved, he provided inspirational guidance.

There is a potential to involve the whole community in the education of children. This is a unique thing. It is a departure from most people sending kids off to the school and trusting local educators. If everyone feels they

*have a hand in education, it will lead to a lot stronger support for educa-
tion in the local schools—if everyone has some degree of ownership.
(Fontaine, 2000)*

The first principle is: *Maximize ownership through partnerships.* Each
CO-SEED site winds up being a partnership between a higher education institution, schools, diverse community organizations, and an
environmental learning center. The community organizations may be
the historical society, the conservation commission, the department
of transportation, or the planning board. Environmental centers may
be the zoo, a local trails group, or a regional nature center.

Our second player is Rick Nannicelli, principal of the Great Brook
Middle School. Rick's emphasis on creating a positive climate of student responsibility and mutual respect was one of the preconditions
that attracted us to Great Brook. And his vision of where the project
could take the school was music to our ears.

*My vision for the next five years is to see education outside of the
walls of the school and to see the walls of the school transformed. I want to
see kids do something important for themselves, for the community and the
environment. (Fontaine, 2000)*

The second principle is: *Engage students in real-world projects in the
local environment and the community.* Whether it be rebuilding the ropes
course that got destroyed in the tornado or producing community
recycling brochures for the mayor's office, students can make real
contributions.

CO-SEED and other large-scale projects use an assortment of
strategies to enact these principles in their schools and communities.
For small-scale projects in classrooms or single schools, any one of
these strategies, or even parts of strategies, will get you moving in the
right direction.

Strategy #1: Put an Environmental Educator in
Every School

Just like the 1928 campaign promise to put a chicken in every pot,
we put an environmental educator in every school even though it's
often just a half-time staff person from a local environmental learning

center. In some cases it grows naturally into a full-time position. The environmental educator doesn't just take care of injured birds or take students on nature walks while the classroom teacher gets a coffee break. The environmental educator does some direct teaching and also serves as a kind of librarian of the out-of-doors, connecting teachers to curriculum materials and local resources. Other roles for the environmental educator include acting as:

- **a science and local history expert**, providing classroom teachers with technical information and access to primary source materials on local history, and the demonstration of scientific testing techniques.
- **an outreach coordinator**, providing assistance in contacting community resource people and identifying appropriate locations for field trips, study sites, and community-based programs.
- **a communicator**, providing written documentation of project activities for school and community publications.
- **a standards consultant and curriculum coordinator**, providing specialized knowledge of the state curriculum frameworks and working with teachers to figure out the best ways to use the school grounds and community to teach their existing curriculum.

It's important to help teachers understand that we're not trying to introduce new curriculum; we don't come with a prefab set of activities or an agenda. When teachers complain "Not one more thing to cover!" we try to clarify that the environmental educator is an in-house staff-support person. In Gilford, Assistant Principal Sandy McGonagle recently reported:

> *We've just started to implement FOSS, our new science curriculum, and the teachers were feeling hemmed in and like they had to follow it word for word. Alan (the environmental educator) has helped them see how they can do many of the activities using local resources and they feel freed up because they've got someone to work with.*

The environmental educator offers a breath of fresh air, literally and figuratively.

We encourage the environmental educators to be responsive to teachers' needs and to bring their own magic and interests into the mix. In the Zoo Club at the Beebe School, Stone Zoo's Kim Kezar uses her animal training background to help students make behavior-enrichment toys for parrots, warthogs, and porcupines. Trailmaster Dave Dernbach's knowledge of trail maintenance provided great service-learning options for the Town Forest Day in Gorham. The Harris Center's Beth Frost translated her fascination with traditional culture into a Quebec bread oven project at Great Brook. The oven is now used to bake specialty breads for a student-run business. The Hulbert Outdoor Center's Steve Glazer's interest in local history inspired ten new historical Valley Quests (student and teacher–created educational treasure hunts) in conjunction with historical societies in the Rivendell District. Audubon's Alan MacIntyre brought his ornithology background to bear in helping 22 of the 30 classrooms at Gilford Elementary research and design birdhouses for birds found within the local watershed.

Strategy #2: Create SEED Teams to Provide Vision and Guidance

The SEED team has two or three teachers, an administrator, the environmental educator, a higher education facilitator, two to three community members (not only parents), a school staff person (great to have the maintenance director or the school lunch coordinator), and one or two middle or high school students. These team members are the movers and shakers, those willing to join the fray and rope in others.

The SEED Team meets on a monthly basis, designs in-service professional development offerings, helps to organize the Community Vision to Action forum (more below), prioritizes curriculum initiatives, and communicates with the community through articles in local papers, presentations at school board meetings, and school newsletters. The objective is to turn team members into funders by giving them the purse strings for a mini-grant program within the schools.

When we were in the initial stages of our place-based education initiatives, I met with Zenobia Barlow, the director of the Center for Ecoliteracy in Berkeley, California. (The Center for Ecoliteracy is responsible for a raft of ground-breaking projects in the San Francisco Bay area and their publications such as *Ecoliteracy: Mapping the Terrain* form the bedrock of ecological teaching.) With characteristic Zen simplicity she advised, "If you want to change schools, offer them money to do what you want them to do."

With this guidance in mind, we give money to the SEED teams and say, "Decide what you want to have happen and then offer teachers funds to do these kinds of things." Each SEED team gets from $2,500 to $4,000 to distribute to teachers who request funding for projects to link school, community, and the environment. Teachers apply to the SEED team for mini-grants to purchase snowshoes or field guides or garden tools, hire guest speakers, publish trail guides, or for other activities which will make a project come to fruition. The SEED team determines which projects have the greatest likelihood to improve academic achievement while also benefiting the community and environment. The process of deciding who should get how much funding is one of the best techniques for helping SEED team members bond and gain clarity about what constitutes effective place-based education in their community.

In Gorham, New Hampshire, the SEED Team (locally known as the CEEC Team, short for Community Environmental Education Committee—a new finch) developed a simple grant application form. Among other things, the form asks teachers:

- What will the outcomes of this project be for Gorham students, teachers, and the community?
- How will your project result in a change that will help the local environment?

Notice that the team's goals of having projects reach out from the school into the community and the local environment are clearly articulated in their questions.

In the interstate Rivendell District, the trials and tribulations of dissolving four school districts and creating one new district across state lines have been massive. Last year there was a 120 percent turnover of lead administrators! But the silver lining has been the opportunity to create organizations that emphasize community connectedness within the structure of the administration. In Rivendell, the SEED team has transmuted into the Community Resources Council, which aims to link community resources with the needs of the school. Using a process called the *non-box system*, the council assesses proposals on the basis of both their educational effectiveness and their potential for community-building. In a variation on another old maxim, the goal of these SEED teams is: Feed two birds with one hand.

Strategy #3: Build Connections through Community Vision to Action Forums

The Vision to Action Forum is a one-and-a-half-day meeting, Friday evening through Saturday afternoon, for a broad cross-section of community members. Optimally, the forum engages 100 to 200 people in identifying what they love about their community and what challenges they face. Then, after a process of prioritization, action committees are formed to address the three to five most salient issues. Projects that emerge might include creating a local newsletter, preserving open space, developing better afterschool recreational opportunities, or creating better relationships between the police and local youth.

The SEED team takes the lead in planning for the forum, which takes about six months to organize. Twenty community members are trained as facilitators, and they also invite people to come and serve as hosts. David Dernbach of Trailmaster from Randolph, New Hampshire, recommends including the broadest range of political points of view, "from the greenest of greens to the blue smoke crowd." Similarly, Nick Donahue, New Hampshire Commissioner of Education, suggests that community engagement is strengthened when you seek out unlikely partnerships. (Remember the Strange Bedfellows Principle!) At the end of a recent leadership seminar, he encouraged a group of funders and educators "to take an old boy to lunch." Birdwatchers and snowmobilers might discover that they agree on trail development in town. After serving as a facilitator during a community forum in Gorham, New Hampshire, Sasha Letellier, a high school junior, offered the following reflection:

> *Before I was involved as a facilitator for the Community Gathering, I would walk down the street and adults looked at me like I was some trouble-causing kid. Now when I walk down the street, adults that I didn't know before say hi to me, stop me to tell me what a great job I did and talk to me about the conversations of that weekend.*

When we conduct the forums in our CO-SEED communities, education issues emerge, but the focus is not exclusively on education. Our objective is to initiate community projects and then look for ways to connect action committees with school curriculum. Here are two illustrative examples.

At Four Futures: Common Threads, a multitown Community Vision to Action Forum in April 2000 for the towns of the Rivendell district, the idea surfaced to unify the towns with a recreational trail. Two members of the SEED team decided to spearhead organizing and grantwriting for the trail. Their efforts resulted in $40,000 of funding from both the Vermont and New Hampshire Trails programs, the first time the two groups have ever jointly funded a project.

The Cross-Rivendell Trail Project has attracted an active committee of school and community members. Some classes have begun to investigate possible locations for segments of the trail. Work is underway to design curriculum units around trail research, design, and construction, and a paid student summer work crew has been launched. A Trail Project kick-off dinner in May 2001 attracted 40 local landowners and elected officials who enthusiastically offered their support. In the room were many citizens who had previously been skeptical about the creation of the new multistate school district.

In urban Malden, Massachusetts, our January 2001 forum focused primarily on the Beebe School neighborhood and parent community. But since the Beebe forum was such a success, forums for each of the other four magnet schools and a citywide forum are being considered for the future. At the forum, Malden Mayor Richard Howard said:

> One of the things we want to prioritize over the coming years is an effort to bring the outside community into education and into the school community, and we're putting a big push on especially the business sector to match up with a school in any way they see fit.

At the Beebe School, this year's schoolwide theme is Malden: Our History, Our Environment, Our Health. One recent project has been the study of nearby Fellsmere Pond. In planning for this year, when the possibility of conducting field studies of the Malden River was proposed, many of the teachers asked, "What river?" The river is so channeled and hemmed in by old industrial facilities it is almost invisible to many residents. Enter John Pereira of Combined

Properties, the force behind Telecom City, a massive brownfields commercial redevelopment project along the Malden River. When he heard about the mayor's charge and the school's focus on local studies, he realized that he could both improve public relations and meet the school's needs by educating teachers about the river and his project. In June 2001, a boat trip on the Malden River, paid for by Pereira, was the central component of a professional development program for teachers on how to use the river as a curricular theme for the following school year.

The recurrent theme here is: Enhance the synergy between active learning and smart growth. Community forums build bridges between school improvement, community vitality, and environmental quality. Commenting on our work in Antrim, John Vance, executive director of Monadnock Business Ventures stated:

> *It's been fascinating to observe the synergy between the changes at the Great Brook School in Antrim and the community development initiatives in town. The Plan New Hampshire Charette, the Celtic Festival, and the redevelopment of the Chicago Cutlery Mill all go hand in hand with Great Brook being named New Hampshire Middle School of the Year.*

In this case, the two birds are feeding each other!

Strategy #4: Tread Lightly When You Carry a Green Stick

Environmental education often raises people's hackles. Michael Sanera and Jane Shaw, in their critique of environmental education entitled *Facts, Not Fear*, contends that environmental educators are short on facts and long on cultivating unnecessary fear. And they suggest that these educators are too often advocates for causes rather than objective educators, considering the many sides of complex issues. You're bound to run into this perspective if you advocate for environmental or place-based education in your town.

When we approached the Gorham, New Hampshire, community about their potential interest in CO-SEED, a segment of the community was strongly opposed. One community member said that Antioch New England "promoted the teachings of environmental groups, and that some information being taught in schools today is little more than propaganda." In correspondence with the senior vice president of Crown Vantage Paper Company, one of the primary employers in northern New Hampshire, we got a clear articulation of the community concern:

> *Folks parading under the banner of environmentalism are greeted with suspicion and mistrust in the North Country. In the last ten or fifteen years, the more radical environmentalists appear to have adopted an "ends justify the mean" approach to correcting what they perceive as society's environmental problems. In the process, they have run roughshod over many values held dear here: unbiased science, Yankee independence, and economic livelihood. The frequent refrain is that "environmentalists" would like to lock up the North Country so the city-dwellers will have a place to vacation—without regard to the economic impact on those who live here.*

The problem stemmed from our partnership with the Appalachian Mountain Club, which had intervened in dam relicensing hearings in the previous five years, generating much ill will. The AMC's actions had both hampered the operations of the local paper industry and led to costly legal proceedings. We were guilty by association. Our challenge was to develop a strategy that respected the various perspectives in the community and to find a form of environmental education that honored local economic and ecological realities.

In the beginning, the CO-SEED materials talked about educating for "ecological literacy," which for many in the North Country translated into tree hugging. They assumed we wanted to teach children that cutting down trees was bad and that by extension, people that cut down trees (their parents) were also bad. (I can sympathize. It's like when my kids come home after the substance abuse program in school and tell me I shouldn't drink a beer with dinner.) In southern and central New Hampshire, "ecological literacy" played well, but not up north. In Gorham, the solution was to focus on forestry education. We worked with the town forester, placed an intern in the school who owned his own independent logging operation, and implemented a high school science curriculum that focused on the town forest.

By having AMC educators work in the schools and collaborate on forestry education, and by providing opportunities for people from different factions to work together on shared projects, the social climate has improved. Commenting on the change in temperature, Appalachian Mountain Club vice president Walter Graff noted, "Prior to CO-SEED, our staff were afraid to shop in Gorham wearing any piece of clothing adorned with an AMC logo. Now they're proud to wear their AMC fleeces and it often leads to constructive conversations in the check-out line."

A group of educators in Montana had a similar experience a few years ago. When they tried to implement a statewide environmental education program, they found that "environmental education" was a lead balloon. But when they talked about a Montana Cultural Heritage program, there was support across the board. The program explores the history of people's relationship with the land just the way an environmental education program would, but "cultural heritage" has less baggage than "environmental education," and places environmental issues within a broader context. Similarly, we have found it more effective to talk about "place-based education" rather than "ecological literacy." Sometimes, we elaborate and refer to "community- and place-based education," to give equal emphasis to cultural and natural contexts for learning.

For me, environmental education is like cilantro. Cilantro is an appealing herb when used in the right proportion. Salsa with too much cilantro is obtrusive and unpalatable. But salsa without cilantro doesn't taste right; it's missing an essential ingredient. In community- and place-based education we need to find the same kind of balance between environmental quality and economic vitality, or between nature studies, history, and literature

In CO-SEED schools, we try to create this kind of balance in a variety of ways. We encourage SEED teams to pursue projects within four domains of work: curriculum integration, schoolyard enhancement, community-based education, and school sustainability. A thread of environmentalism runs through all of these, but doesn't dominate in any of them. In each domain we seek to balance environmental perspectives with other genuine concerns. The following text details each of these domains.

Curriculum integration. We try hard not to get labeled as just a science education initiative. Some of the best school/community projects, for example, focus on community history. The Community Arts Day in Antrim, New Hampshire, brings stonecutters, glassblowers, contra dance musicians, African drummers, and weavers into the school to share their passions. We like it when the middle school math teacher has the seventh and eighth graders survey the fifth and sixth graders about the school lunch program and the afterschool club offerings because they are using the school for real-life data analysis. Other projects integrate art and science, such as when the art teacher joins up with the fifth grade teachers to create accurate, elegant, and artistic maps of the wildlife at the local McCabe Forest.

Schoolyard enhancement. The National Wildlife Federation has helped many schools improve habitat for wildlife in their schoolyards. Butterfly gardens, native plantings that feed birds, and model ecosystem plantings all make the schoolgrounds more biodiverse. But we want the schoolyard to be more welcoming for people too. We encourage the creation of suitable outdoor workspaces so teachers can send children outside to write comfortably in their journals, or so parents have better seating at athletic events. The Boston Schoolyards Initiative works with neighborhood groups to design schoolyards that serve as community gathering spots.

Last spring, Bill Church, the high school physics teacher in Littleton, New Hampshire, was rebuilding a set of steps on a trail that connects the schoolgrounds with downtown. He commented, "Because of CO-SEED, I felt comfortable calling up the Town Public Works Director at 6:30 in the morning to request a front-end loader to deliver rocks to the upper end of the trail. He was there at 7:15." Place-based education is about connecting people to people, as well as connecting people to nature.

Community-based education. Collaborating with the hardware store to help them assemble their wheelbarrows is equally as valuable as completing a project with the town conservation commission. In the new Depot Project, a place-based program based at the Great Brook Middle School, serving the towns of Antrim, Hancock, Francestown, and Bennington, New Hampshire, students designed and built the new entranceway garden for the town selectmen's office. In Malden, Massachusetts, when the city recognized that they were recycling only three-and-a-half percent of their solid waste, the mayor said, "Beebe's our environmental school, let's get some of those students involved in helping us solve this problem." All sectors of the community can provide opportunities for useful service-learning projects for the school.

School sustainability. Examining the school as an integrated system offers numerous opportunities for balancing economic and envi-

Place-based education is about connecting people to people, as well as connecting people to nature.

ronmental points of view. Students can research whether using 100 percent postconsumer waste paper in our copiers is worth the cost. Energy assessments can lead to a reduction of the school's electrical bills as well as provide good math curriculum. Monitoring of indoor air quality makes for good science education at the middle and high school levels and can potentially reduce the incidence of respiratory infections during the winter months. Encouraging parent-led groups to bike to school can reduce air pollution on the schoolgrounds and increase physical fitness. A balanced emphasis on health, ecology, and economy makes these kinds of activities broadly appealing.

Wild Treasures, an Antioch New England program for Vermont and New Hampshire middle schools, provides a further example of the cilantro balance we aspire to. Environmental studies faculty member Jimmy Karlan designed this program to encourage middle school teachers and students to research ways to make their school more ecologically sustainable. Once the research is complete, students propose changes to the school board, and, if approved, help implement them. One sixth grade class at the Oak Grove School in Brattleboro, Vermont, evaluated the school lunch program. An early summary of the student research, written by the students, explains:

> *The projects we chose to explore are starting a schoolwide composting and garden project, a paper waste recycling program, and finding an alternative for polystyrene lunch trays. The main questions we used were: How much paper, lunch trays and food waste do we have in one day, one week, one year…? We found that we waste about 20,350 trays, 5,106 pounds of paper, and 5,735 pounds of food waste in one year. We need improvement! With polystyrene lunch trays, we are still debating whether to get an industrial sized dishwasher for the plastic trays or the biodegradable trays with less maintenance.*

When they interviewed school officials about the dishwasher option, they discovered cost and logistical hurdles, which led them to suggest replacing the polystyrene trays with paper trays, which can be recycled or composted.

In April 2001, their proposal to the school board was approved unanimously. One school board member recommended implementing the change at all of Brattleboro's schools rather just this one elementary school. School superintendent Ray McNulty commented, "I was really impressed with the data collection and the work that went into it." Significantly, the school board appreciated that the students made a case that was both financially reasonable *and* ecologically responsible.

Similarly, high school students in a Rural Trust project in South Dakota did economic research on the problem of decreasing sales tax revenues in their town. A growing number of local residents were shopping out of town because local stores didn't carry the products they were looking for. The students found that if these residents would spend an additional 15 percent of their income in town, rather than shopping elsewhere, the community could be economically healthy. Through working with local merchants to diversify their offerings, and educating the citizenry about the impact of shopping locally, students have been credited with increasing those sales tax revenues by 27 percent, or $7,000,000. Paul Nachtigal, past Director of the Rural Challenge, says, "By raising those issues, by surfacing that conversation in the broader community, these students have contributed directly to the viability of that community." (Baldwin, 1998)

Place-based education works best when both economic and environmental concerns are balanced. In Alaska, that means inviting native elders to train adolescents in caribou hunting. In Brooklyn, New York, that means having students map the sources of toxic waste emissions to help in the struggle to reduce childhood asthma. In the North Country of New Hampshire, it means teaching math and science through forestry education. Environmental education gains credibility when jobs are given the same importance as prairie dogs and plovers.

Strategy #5: Nurture Continuous Improvement through Ongoing Professional Development

In the beginning, it will be easy to attract the early adopters, the handful of teachers who share your beliefs and want to move in the same direction. On the other end of the spectrum are the sticks-in-the-mud. Their lives are too full, they don't see the relevance to what they're doing, or they are just a couple of years away from retirement. Don't worry about them. Your challenge is to get to that broad middle group of teachers who are recruitable but hesitant, and for lots of good reasons. One of the big tricks is: *Just show up.* More often than not, it's the chance conversation in the hallway or the visit to the teaching intern that leads to a blossoming of interest in the program among new teachers. And your presence shows that you are committed to the project and willing to work hard to involve others.

Getting involved in a place-based education program is a form of professional development for teachers—and it's often difficult to get overworked teachers to volunteer for professional development. It's helpful to approach professional development keeping in mind that old marketing adage that says "the customer needs four or five exposures to the product before she'll buy it." Professional development needs to happen in many guises over long periods of time. Rather than try to create new committees or schedule new meetings, try to piggyback onto existing structures. The practice of piggybacking can make it easier to get new teachers involved and give staying power to long-term efforts. The following are some of the venues we utilize to conduct professional development.

In-service workshops. Schools have a few in-service days built into their contracts and we try to claim some of them for programs on place-based education. During the second year at Great Brook School, we offered an all-day program called "Machinations, Magellan and McCabe: Problem Solving in the Local Environment," which featured workshops on design technology, orienteering, snowshoe explorations, and mapmaking. All of these workshops translated into new projects over the next two years. In Malden, we conducted a Faculty Visioning Day in the summer, followed by a full-day professional development program in the fall. The Visioning Day parallels the Community Vision to Action forum that we conduct, but it was just for school staff, administrators, and teachers. We're considering adding a visioning day for students as well in some of our new sites.

Our recent winter staff development day in Gilford, entitled "The Power of Place: Digging into the Local Community," was consciously designed to be both playful and serious. One of the goals for the year was to have students and teachers "play and learn in their backyard," so we created a set of indoor/outdoor opportunities. We created treasure hunts on the playground, learned math through measuring trees and identifying tracks, constructed historical quests, refined the school's recycling program, and trained teachers to use GPS units.

We also take advantage of regular faculty meetings to make presentations on research studies, to conduct problem-solving activities, and to do evaluation with teachers. Voluntary book groups that read and discuss books like *Starting from Scratch* (Levy, 1999) or *Digging Deeper: Integrating Youth Gardens into Schools and Communities* (Kiefer and Kemple, 1998) also raise the level of conversation.

Grade-level team meetings. This is where most of the planning happens in schools, and we soon realized that it was a venue we should use. When the district science curriculum was reorganized and the sixth grade teachers at Great Brook needed to teach geology, we did a mini-workshop on connecting the New Hampshire curriculum guidelines with projects that used local resources. The crucial learning for us was that we had to go to the teachers rather than expecting them to come to us.

In Gilford, Alan MacKenzie, the Audubon environmental educator in the schools, conducted an all-day program just for the first, second, and third grade teachers on how to use the nature trail. This close focus on particular grade levels and a specific topic facilitated lots of quick curriculum development.

Teacher retreats and summer institutes. Research by the Chesapeake Bay Foundation concluded that short-term teacher trainings didn't translate into better environmental teachers or improved student behaviors in school. They now have a two-day minimum for curriculum trainings and most of their teacher workshops are a week long. Also, they realized that residential training programs intimidated teachers who weren't early adopters, so they decided to offer multiday, but not overnight, programs closer to the urban areas where many teach.

In CO-SEED institutes, we aspire to a healthy balance of work and play. Our summer institute includes mini-courses on mapmaking, teaching to the standards, and teaching local history, as well as yoga, swimming hole excursions, nighttime games of "vampire orienteering tag," and alpine flora field trips. We've also found that it's crucial to include high school students and community members as participants in our institutes. The enthusiasm of the high school students often overcomes the hesitancy of jaded teachers. At a retreat in Gorham, one of the best project ideas came from a high school student who said, "You know, one of the really big problems [at our school] is that it's too buggy at the field where the girls' lacrosse team practices." This comment led to a wonderful, integrated industrial-arts-and-ecology project on making bat boxes—to increase the bat population, to eat the mosquitoes, and to make lacrosse practice more enjoyable.

Turn teachers into workshop leaders. Teachers listen to other teachers. My colleague Heidi Watts found that the single most effective instrument for professional development is having teachers visit each other's classrooms. When a teacher sees that another teacher can do something, she's more willing to try it herself. If visits are not practical, then have teachers lead workshops. Once you've identified the teachers and community members who have classroom skills and charisma, get them on the team. We have teachers from our established sites do workshops for teachers from new sites.

Develop grantwriting skills in lead teachers and administrators. After your own involvement with the project ends, you want things to keep going. One of the ways this can happen is if teachers and environmental learning center staff take on the challenge of seeking external funding to support ongoing innovation. We help teachers learn how to write grants and help them get their articles about their work into print. To date, our support of local school districts has led to more than $600,000 in new grants and leveraged funds to support place-based education projects in these schools.

Strategy #6: Nurture Community Exchange

Once community engagement begins, there's a need for institutionalized structures that keep the energy flowing back and forth from school to community. This is new territory for us and for lots of place-based education projects around the country. In the search for new species of school/community engagement, we are exploring these possibilities:

Educator membership on town committees. One way to maintain the flow of connections between school and community and to keep teachers abreast of local issues is to have teachers and environmental educators serve on town committees. Because environmental educator Beth Frost is a member of the conservation commission in Hancock, New Hampshire (one of Great Brook's sending towns), she's been able to involve middle school students in a trail project to connect the school with a new recreation area. In our new site in Bradford, Vermont, we've got a selectman and a conservation commissioner on the SEED Team, and Heather Trillium, the environmental educator from the Hulbert Outdoor Center, makes it part of her job to attend town committee meetings.

Curriculum exhibition events. Public events that bring students, teachers, and parents together to view the curriculum give community members a formal chance to see what place-based education offers. Curriculum work that impacts the neighborhood and the environment deserves to be celebrated in the same way we celebrate theatrical and sports events. In Gilford, New Hampshire, we took advantage of the school's monthly curriculum showcase to present the improved community access to the nature trail. On family math and science nights in Malden, Massachusetts, students and parent volunteers taught community members about how school programs contribute to improvements at the Stone Zoo. In Antrim, New Hampshire, the annual Great Brook Junk Out, a Saturday cleanup of the downtown stream, was an extension of the fifth grade wetlands curriculum.

We also encourage the use of town committees as juries to evaluate student work. When Great Brook sixth and seventh graders developed a plan for a piece of conservation land, the students presented their work to the members of the conservation commission for approval. The review of the students' plan also constitutes professional development for community members who serve on the commission.

Community Arts Day. What a great idea! All regular classes are canceled for the day and community artists and craftspeople come to the school to lead half-day and all-day workshops. Local potters do clay work, stone masons teach stone carving, and the environmental educator does snow sculpture. One year, the industrial arts teacher and I made snow forts with the wind-packed snow. It was a thrill to watch half-a-dozen fifth and sixth graders muscle a hundred-pound block of snow onto the roof of our entrance tunnel. One of the most popular classes was Rock 'n' Roll Rebels. Musicians from the locally famous Rynborn Blues Club worked with students to craft a couple of songs. Later this project evolved into cutting a CD with some middle school musicians.

At the end of the day, we thanked the community members with high tea, complete with porcelain teacups, Twinings, crustless cream-cheese-and-cucumber sandwiches, scones with strawberry jam. The atmosphere was buoyant. "I always love coming into this school," declared one musician, "because the atmosphere is always so upbeat. It really feels like teachers and students want to be here." These kinds of responses are the foundation stones of community support.

Community engagement evenings. Another vehicle for extending community engagement can be evening dinner meetings with selected segments of the community. Because many of our projects used town libraries and primary source material, we invited town librarians and members of town historical societies to join us for dinner and problem solving. Teachers and students presented relevant projects and then broke into small groups to talk about how the libraries and historical societies could help us and how students could be a resource in their work. Could students create exhibitry for town libraries? Could class projects focus on data collection for the historical archives? Could the town librarians help students do research that contributes to the local Celtic festival? Out of one of these meetings emerged a project in which sixth graders documented the history of individual houses for the historic society.

Another evening focused on local craftspeople and artists, and another on town businesspeople and community leaders. Our meeting with local artists led to the idea of a residency by a landscape designer to work on a design for Great Brook's schoolyard. Twenty-four fifth-through-eighth graders participated in the month-long project to create the master plan—a plan that will guide class and community involvement for the next five years.

By implementing pieces of these six strategies consistently over a number of years, your school and community will start to look different. The process can be likened to the geological concept of punctuated equilibrium, which suggests that change happens little by little over a long period of time and then, all at once, there's a major shift. Or maybe it's like moving past the tipping point on a pair of scales—you don't see much change, and then the balance shifts to the other side. My advice: Don't get frustrated in the early stages. Assume a time frame of three to five years at a minimum, and learn to love the process as much as the product.

Classroom Walls Opening Wide

Just as we advocate for children learning from elders in their communities, it's important that we also hear directly from teachers. Listen to the voices of some of the teachers in CO-SEED schools who are leading the charge in changing schools.

A Stroll through Antrim's Changing Landscape

Anne Kenney and Barbara Black, fifth grade teachers at Great Brook Middle School, love the process. Anne was about to retire a few years ago, but she got so excited about the Wetlands project that she and Barbara had initiated, she can't make herself leave. It's exciting to hear teachers describe their work from the inside out.

Anne and Barbara used a Stories in the Land Fellowship from The Orion Society to engage fifth graders in creating a historic walking tour of the center of Antrim, New Hampshire. Their elegant guidebook recently won a special achievement award from the New Hampshire Preservation Alliance for its fine integration of curriculum and historic preservation. The following description by Anne and Barbara of their year-long project captures the spirit of embedding classroom learning in the life of the community.

Lauren gazed confidently over the hushed audience of senior citizens, parents, volunteers, interested citizens, and fifth graders assembled in the historic Presbyterian Church on Antrim's Main Street. Eyes sparkling with anticipation, she stood at the podium ready to retrace the twisting path students and teachers had followed to reach this celebration day, June 9, 2000. Sitting in their pews, nervous with anticipation, classmates waited for Lauren to begin.

"Welcome to all our interviewees, volunteers, family, and friends…" The celebration had begun.

What had happened since that September day when forty-three fifth graders from Antrim and three surrounding communities first entered our two classrooms at Great Brook School? A strange school, unknown teachers, the exciting possibility of new friends and new learning opportunities awaited students. Classroom walls would open wide into the surrounding Antrim community as we explored the changing landscape of Antrim's South Village. What would this year-long exploration look like? We did not know the exact route, but students and teachers together would investigate the landscape and learn together. The final product of the yearlong study would be a guidebook containing a walking tour of South Village. We had the vision, but not the stops along the way. Those would evolve as we learned the stories in the land.

The two classes brainstormed places of interest in the four communities in which they live and created lists of places they might include on a hometown tour. Students composed a letter and sent it to longtime and new Antrim residents. This survey letter asked what places in Antrim would the letter reader take a visitor, who are the local "experts," and if the resident would be willing to be interviewed for the project....

In October and November, students and teachers met with the professional photographer who is our consultant. We learned photography techniques and what characteristics a worthwhile photo has. In small groups, we toured downtown Antrim and snapped photos of places that might be on our tour....

We were ready to commence the history component of the project. The teachers consulted with New Hampshire history scholar Dr. R. Stuart Wallace. In early December...he introduced fifth graders to historical research by using hands on activities that stressed a variety of ways to gather information. During the winter, he led students through discussions and activities that enhanced their understanding of New Hampshire history, the styles and architectural features of New England buildings, and the changing landscapes of New England towns and villages....

In April, decisions were made about what buildings deserved to be included in the walking tour of South Village.... Kermit Davis, a guest speaker much favored by the children, enthralled them by sharing his father's diary entries written about life in Antrim one hundred years ago. The Antrim Historical Society generously allowed us to borrow archival written resources and photographs. The written material was sometimes difficult. Therefore, adult volunteers often read and discussed with the two students involved in researching a building....

Excuse my interruption, but I feel compelled to provide some liner notes. I have worked with both of these teachers over a number of years and I never cease to be amazed at their ability to engage students at each step in a project that is constantly evolving. The teachers knew they wanted to create a historical interpretive guide, but they left it up to the community and the students to determine which sites would be presented. Appropriate letter construction, good penmanship, correct spelling—the language arts component—were all part of the early stages of connecting with the community. The teachers also treated the students like respected colleagues and connected them with real community experts, such as Stuart Wallace, a noted New Hampshire historian. With the support of these teachers, students did not only the primary source research (an integral part of the New Hampshire social studies curriculum guidelines) but also the original photography for the guidebook.

It was also time to start the oral histories, each focusing on a particular building. Antrim's senior citizens are repositories of local folklore and history. Students needed their stories, but first they had to acquire interviewing techniques. Lyman Gilmore, a local oral historian, shared his expertise with our interviewers. Students then used that knowledge to write questions to use while practicing their interviewing skills on a friend, a mom or dad, and an older family member....

The Maplehurst Inn, built two hundred years ago in South Village, was still cloaked in the morning shadows. Student oral historians clutched their interview questions. In pairs they had already set up tape recorders and adjusted microphones set on dining room tables in three separate areas. White table clothes gleamed and so did the interviewers who were dressed in Sunday best out of respect for their senior citizens interviewees. Our first interviewee stepped in. Two students came forward, "Good morning, I am Conrad and this is Alex. May we escort you to our table?"

The tapes became a vital part of classroom resource material. Students listened to them, took notes to include in their research, shared facts that applied to other students' buildings and noted discrepancies between interviews.... Our historians had to decide which story, if any, should be given credence. Definitely a real-life problem.

In May, both classes focused on writing the guidebook. First, the two experts on a building each wrote his/her own description based on joint research. They rewrote to include the best parts of both pieces. After reviews by the teachers, students rechecked facts, clarified language, edited, and made phone calls to verify information. This was a long process that required continuous rereading and revisions....

Our research took other forms. One class walked downtown armed with measuring tools. Intent on a real measuring lesson based on math skills learned in the classroom, they measured buildings, focusing on ascertaining size. The other class sat on the village sidewalk across from their buildings and used skills learned in art class to sketch it....

It's impressive to see students actually doing history rather than learning history. So much of the time, history is presented to students as a predigested set of facts and dates. Here, students become the historians. They have to deal with the conflicts between interviews and journal recollections; they have to create chronologies of events; they have to become journalists—writing and rewriting, checking facts with their sources, deciding whether it's acceptable to rephrase a direct quote. Math becomes not just workbook problems but an integral part of the project at hand; art has a purpose.

> *The big day arrived. The Presbyterian Church was an appropriate setting for our celebration since Antrim's first settlers were predominantly Presbyterians. Student editors stepped in turn to the microphone, and each traces a part of the path we followed from fall to spring. Each of the student research partners briefly highlighted the value of their interviewee's information and presented a floral tribute, a thank you note, and a photo taken at the interview. After this brief ceremony, everybody adjourned to the church hall where students conducted a tour of the village using student posters on easels of each building. On display were all of our resources and—best of all—a copy of the walking tour guidebook* [Author's note: This fine booklet is equal in quality to many professionally produced historical society publications.]
>
> *How have their learning experiences changed our students? Students are much more aware of the need to preserve history and stories for later generations. They realize that there are mysteries to solve.... Taking notes when we have speakers has become more important to them because they now realize the need to refer back to these notes when doing later investigations and writing. They know the importance of getting permission to use copyrighted materials, such as maps and music on tape. Because they listened to and took notes from their taped interviews, they are well versed in closely checking the data on tape and discovering discrepancies. Perhaps the learning most valuable to the society in which they live is a deeper understanding of the community's elders as respected sources of knowledge and as really nice people. Just being comfortable around senior citizens was newly acquired learning for some of our students.*

> *We and our students have gained much by using the community as a*
> *classroom, its citizens as experts, and primary sources as textbooks. This*
> *immersion into a sense of place and community helped us develop interdis-*
> *ciplinary lessons that made learning meaningful for students. Digging into*
> *the layers of Antrim's history and searching for the clues left on the land*
> *has helped students value community and recognize its continuous evolu-*
> *tion over time. (Fontaine, 2001)*

As I finish reading this, my throat tightens and tears come to my eyes.
This feels right to me—this is what school is supposed to be. Let me
see if I can articulate the crucial elements. The students and teachers
here were all involved in *solving a real problem*: the preserving of history and the publication of a useful document for the town. In the
process, they became creators, not just consumers, of knowledge. The
teachers fostered an atmosphere of *shared commitment*—each student
had a distinct, important job, and many parent volunteers, discipline
experts, local business people, and senior citizens got swept up in
making the project happen. The students developed *articulated skills*,
and the teachers knew how to scaffold activities so that practice
made perfect. The students did numerous practice interviews before
doing the real ones. No slapdash efforts here—each piece of work
was refined. There was an attentive *nearness to beauty* in many of the
details of the process—the white tablecloths and Sunday best for the
interviews, flowers and photos for the community participants, the
elegance of the final publication. And finally, there was a *community
audience*, at the Presbyterian Church and among all the users of the
tour guide. The guides are so popular, they've already had to do a
second printing. And the impact on the community? As Barbara and
Anne commented in their description of the project, "Townspeople
are overwhelmed! People are amazed that fifth graders can do this."

We've completed our involvement in the CO-SEED project in
Antrim after our original three-year commitment, but many aspects
of the initiative live on. Just the other day I had a conversation with
one of the selectmen who helped to organize the Community Vision
to Action Forum almost five years ago. "You know," he mused, "some
of the things that we started after the forum are just coming to
fruition now. The whole downtown revitalization effort started that
day and now it's really happening." The fifth graders' work con-

tributed to making that revitalization a reality.

The Fellsmere Pond Study at the Beebe School

Just north of Boston, Malden was a shoe city, until shoe manufac-
turing moved south early in the twentieth century. Now it's an ethnically diverse, recovering urban community of about fifty-six thousand. With federal desegregation money, the school department created five magnet schools. One of them is the Beebe Environmental
and Health Sciences Magnet School, a K–8 school with an environmental theme. Beebe is in the heart of the city, not far from the T
station and City Hall. It's surrounded by busy streets, businesses, and
crowded residential areas. Over the past three years, CO-SEED staff
has worked with the administration, faculty, and community to actu-
alize the environmental theme. Just as in Antrim, the teachers have
developed thematic, locally based units that integrate the curriculum
with the community.

The Massachusetts curriculum frameworks designate "community"
as part of the third grade social studies curriculum. It's a concept
that's hard to teach just using a textbook, so the teachers chose
Fellsmere Pond, a city park about a five-minute walk from the
school, as the centerpiece of an integrated unit.

Here's how Robin Jorgenson, a Magnet Program Focus Teacher in
the school, describes the project:

> The teachers wanted the students to learn about community by study-
> ing Fellsmere Pond as a community resource. They wanted students to learn
> the value of the park, ecologically, historically, recreationally and as an impor-
> tant aspect of a healthy community. They also wanted to integrate science,
> math, health, art and technology components. To give back something to the
> community, the students will create a brochure which will show the park's
> history, ecology, recreational activities and include a student made map.
> Students will learn stewardship as they discuss ways they can make a differ-
> ence and plan how to encourage others to help them take care of the park.
>   One of the goals is to have the students learn about the organizations
> in the community, so we asked Frank Russell, president of the Historical
> Society, to discuss the history of Fellsmere Pond. It was interesting for the
> students to learn that Malden had a group of people who cared enough
> about the history of their community to work to preserve it. Mr. Russell was

kind enough to bring us copies of original 1897 and 1910 park commission reports so the students could read primary sources. How exciting for them to read how the early park commissioners valued parks as a community resource also. As we read the park commission's budget, we found that the price of items in the 1890's is a real economic lesson in itself.

The students and teachers here were all involved in solving a real problem.... In the process, they became creators, not just consumers, of knowledge.

© James Tyler/Center for Ecoliteracy

To include math in the unit, the teachers decided to have the students create and distribute surveys of how Beebe families use the park recreationally. They will tabulate data and create tables, and then use the tables to create graphs. Here the work we are doing with the MCAS (the state curriculum test) analysis teams helps us to target our curriculum development. Our analysis team found that Beebe students did very well interpreting line plots and bar graphs, but they had problems with pictographs. Therefore, we are making sure that the students will create pictographs from the data they collect. (Jorgenson, 2001)

The math component of this project is a great example of how place-based learning can increase academic achievement. These third graders will really understand pictographs because they were part of a meaningful project. Similar curriculum enhancements are happening throughout the school. Second graders created a butterfly garden on a tiny patch of city property next to the school, as the final piece of a comprehensive science curriculum. Seventh graders studied the water chemistry at the park and in the Malden River. The middle school students built solar ovens and learned about the potential of solar technology in developing third world countries. History, art, and writing were integrated into the fifth graders' creation of an "urban quest," with support from the National Park Service's Rivers and Trails program.

The urban environment of Malden offers the same opportunities for place-based education as the rural environment of Antrim. In fact, the diversity of partners, neighborhoods, and cultural communities, as well as the nearness-at-hand of resources, almost makes it easier to do place-based education in the city than in the country.

Notes from the Field

Enough from my New England neighbors. Time for a cross-country field trip. Let's take a peek into some of the classrooms, communities, and schools around the country where students are getting back to where they once belonged. From the welter of place-based education initiatives in the United States, I've chosen to visit four bioregional initiatives. In the mid-Atlantic states we'll drop in on the Bay Schools Project of the Chesapeake Bay Foundation and look at what's going on in schools in downtown Baltimore and others in the Bay watershed. Further south we'll visit one of the elementary schools in the Pine Jog Model Schools in Environmental Education Program in Florida. Out west, the Bioregional Outdoor Education Project on the Colorado Plateau of the Four Corners School will take us to canyon country and a school in the high desert. And, like our pioneer forebears, we'll end our journey out on the Pacific Coast in the misty mountains of Northern California, where we'll sample the wares of the North Coast Rural Challenge project in Mendocino County, California.

It's an interesting study in co-evolution to see how these regional collaborations of environmental learning centers, public schools, and higher education institutions have all moved toward similar missions and structures. Yet the local color and character of each bioregion often makes the program content unique. From crabs and wild celery in the Chesapeake to Anasazi pictograms in southern Utah, the subject matter is different, but the commitment to problem solving, community service, and the three Rs is consistent in each place.

Connecting School Improvement with Ecological Restoration in the Bay Schools Project

The Bay Schools Project (BSP) is an initiative of the Chesapeake Bay Foundation. In cooperation with the Maryland State Department of Education, the project works with rural, suburban, and urban school districts throughout Maryland. It includes three elementary schools, one K–8 public school, two middle schools, two high schools, and one pre-K–12 private school.

The appeal of the Bay Schools Project is its clear focus on both school reform and environmental quality in the Chesapeake Bay watershed. The two primary objectives of the project are:

1. to improve student achievement and engagement in learning throughout all subject areas; and
2. to encourage students to act responsibly toward the environment and the Chesapeake Bay. (Bearman, 2001)

The Bay Schools Project grew out of the nationwide study of EIC schools (Environment as an Integrating Context) done by the State Education and Environment Roundtable and out of an evaluation of Chesapeake Bay Foundation (CBF) programs completed in 1999 by evaluators from the University of Michigan.

The evaluation showed that teachers and students are positive about CBF's field and classroom-based programs and that these programs are successful in improving students' attitudes and knowledge about the

David Sobel

Chesapeake Bay, as well as their intention to act in environmentally responsible ways. The evaluation recommended that CBF create an extended, classroom-based program to have greater impact on students' environmentally responsible behavior. [Author's emphasis] *(Bearman, 2001)*

This important idea correlates with the Zelezny study cited earlier. It seems that there's substantial evidence that informal environmental education programs help to change students' environmental attitudes and knowledge and strengthen their *intent* to act in responsible ways. But this isn't enough. Environmental organizations around the country are realizing that to inspire and sustain lasting stewardship behavior, they have to commit themselves to long-term partnerships with school districts. The Chesapeake Bay Foundation is one of the leading regional environmental organizations implementing this idea on a significant scale. (Similarly, Walter Graff, Deputy Director of the Appalachian Mountain Club, proclaimed, "I'm finished with these one shot deals. I want AMC to be doing more extended, in-depth work with schools.")

Now in its third year, the Bay Schools Project provides a site coordinator who spends at least a day a week in the schools and encourages diverse partnerships with community organizations. Students from Broadneck High School in Anne Arundel County worked with the local Barnes and Noble bookstore to offer a public reading of *Shoes, Ships and Sealing Wax*, an oral history project produced by high school students. A partnership with the Maryland Institute of Art helped Morrel Park Elementary/Middle School students in Baltimore create a wetland sculpture garden.

Some teachers connect up with existing restoration projects such as Bay Grasses in Classes and the Student Oyster Corps. Other students and teachers have created native flora gardens, initiated schoolwide waste management systems, cleared and mulched trails to provide safe access to streams and wetlands, and assessed the quality of their school's drinking water. All this contributes to creating a "Bay friendly" curriculum that looks at the watershed connections between their school site and the Bay.

The project offers numerous professional development opportunities for teachers, ranging from in-service workshops on Aligning Field Work with the Maryland State Outcomes and Learning Goals to week-long summer sea-kayaking trips that let teachers live and breathe Bay ecology and economics. For some teachers, it's really making a difference. "I was ready to leave my school," said one teacher, "but I stayed because the Bay Schools Project revitalized my teaching. I am committed to it—plus, I couldn't leave my bluebird trail." (Bearman, 2001)

The Bay Schools Project gains its strength from its up-front focus on connecting school improvement, environmental restoration, and community sustainability. Joe Dodge, a Bay Schools project coordinator working with nine schools in urban Baltimore and surrounding counties, has a knack for making these connections.

For the past three years, Maryland's elementary, middle and high school students have been learning about the importance of Chesapeake Bay grasses with help from the Department of Natural Resources (DNR) and the Chesapeake Bay Foundation (CBF). Bay grasses are a critical part of the Chesapeake Bay ecosystem, serving as the nursery and feeding ground for fish and crabs. While water quality improvements have increased the acreage of bay grasses in recent years, we still are only at a fraction of historic levels. This program helps to jump-start the recovery of grasses in areas where they once flourished. By studying the ecological importance of bay grasses, growing grasses in the classroom and then transplanting them in select areas, students are actively participating in restoration and gaining a sense of stewardship of the Bay.

In Morrell Park, a pre-K through eighth grade school in Baltimore, four middle school teachers participated in the Bay Grasses project last year. Students set up two tanks in the classroom and grow wild celery plants from seed, a critical species of underwater grass that is declining in the Chesapeake. Students design investigations that focus on one variable that affects the growth of the plants (light exposure time, salinity, temperature, or water circulation) and then for six to ten weeks, students monitor the growth of the plants, collect data, and post their findings on the internet. At the end of the growth period, students analyze data and write conclusions before wading into waist-deep water to transplant the seedlings in a local tributary. Morrell Park and other students have grown more than 100,000 wild celery seedlings. And all the diverse experimentation in different classes helps to perfect techniques for growing many species of grasses that will be used throughout Maryland for bay grass restoration projects. (Dodge, 2001)

The elegant aspect of the Bay Schools Project is the intent to develop a "sense of Bay" in urban and rural student alike. The Bay Schools range from being a stone's throw away from the Chesapeake to being a world apart. Some students in Washington, D.C. suburbs have never even seen the Bay. Downtown Baltimore students think that the Bay is just a scenic backdrop for the Orioles' home games at Camden Yards. But, by bringing a little bit of the Bay into the classrooms in the form of salt water aquaria for raising wild celery and oysters, educators get a foot in the door of the students' minds. Through field trips to tributaries and tidal rivers, students and teachers see that their lives and storm drains have a direct effect on the life of the Bay. The Bay is just a step away.

Close-to-home environments also play a role in the Bay Schools curriculum development plans. Joe Dodge continues:

> At Forest Oak Middle School in Gaithersburg, MD, students recently worked with the local power company (PEPCO), the county forestry board and Maryland DNR to plant 60 trees on their schoolyard. The project was the second in a series of plantings with the goal of restoring two acres of stream buffer on the schoolyard to its natural state. Sixty students and ten parent volunteers joined forces with the experts to plant the trees. During the nine weeks prior to the project, students investigated the health of the stream that runs through the schoolyard. They monitored water quality, tested soils, and researched possible ways to correct severe erosion problems along the stream bank. Students demonstrated the ability to meet multiple learning goals during the nine week investigation: they summarized observations; analyzed information from authentic text sources; analyzed directions as they read to perform a task; collected, organized, displayed, and analyzed data; and wrote conclusions to investigations.
>
> At Bohemia Manor Middle School in Cecil County, seventh graders constructed ten rain gardens on the schoolyard to capture rainwater runoff from roof-draining downspouts to reduce erosion and provide habitat for birds and insects. These students are starting to understand that reducing erosion on the schoolyard through creating rain gardens contributes to increased water quality in the Bay which makes it more likely that the wild celery plants they're raising will survive. The pieces of the puzzle are starting to fit together.

Aren't you tired of science experiments that have no connection to the real world? Instead of cutting up dead animals filled with preservatives, Bay Schools students are growing grasses that support the restoration of fish populations in the Bay. And increased fish populations then help sustain the communities threatened by the depletion of marine resources. Increased fish populations also mean job preser-

© James Tyler/Center for Ecoliteracy

Through field trips to tributaries and tidal rivers, students and teachers see that their lives and storm drains have a direct effect on the life of the Bay.

vation, which translates into reduced social services and less likelihood of adolescent drug and alcohol abuse.

It goes back to our update of that old maxim—our strategy is to feed two birds (or perhaps three birds) with the same hand. We're looking for initiatives for school improvement that build on an understanding of systems dynamics. Changes in one part of the system have impacts in other parts of the system. Dissections of dead animals in science class lead to the creation of toxic solid waste that costs the community more in disposal fees. Growing bay grasses in science classes leads eventually to healthier communities, which mean lower health care costs and more wealth to support improved school facilities.

The Nature Conservancy has found a similar dynamic in its work on Block Island, off the coast of Rhode Island. The Nature Conservancy helps to support an educator in the local high school who does science and environmental education focused partially on Conservancy land on the island. But the educator also coaches the basketball team and has taken an active role in working with troubled adolescents on this isolated island. He has endeared himself to many parents through his work in these extracurricular areas. As a result, local citizens have become more supportive of the Nature Conservancy's attempts to protect unique island landscapes. An initiative that begins in the school reaches into the community and generates greater enthusiasm for a conservation agenda.

A parallel feature of the Bay Schools Project is the coordination of the education and environmental agendas at the highest levels of state government. The leadership of the Chesapeake Bay Foundation has been savvy in its creation of alliances between the Maryland State Department of Education and the Department of Natural Resources. Getting different state agencies to work together is another instance of putting systems thinking into action. When the efforts of two agencies support each other, everyone has more energy, and the whole is greater than the sum of its parts. It's like the synergy of running with another person—you are buoyed up and carried along when there's someone running beside you.

Increasing the Academic Performance of Underperforming Schools: Florida's Model Schools in Environmental Education and Accountability Program

The Model Schools program is an initiative of the Pine Jog Environmental Education Center and the Palm Beach County School District. The program works with ten K–5 elementary schools and one middle school. Pine Jog administrators initiated a deeper relationship with local public schools when they realized they weren't realizing their long-term goals.

> *Teachers used to view Pine Jog Environmental Education Center as a daylong field trip, explains Director of Education Susan Toth. "We knew we weren't satisfied to be stand-alone field trips without a real connection to the classroom," she says. So the Center re-thought its mission. (Glenn, 2000)*

Sound familiar? It's interesting to see the convergence on similar kinds of collaborations in all corners of the country. With funding from the MacArthur Foundation, Pine Jog partnered with the Palm Beach County School District to create a set of model schools. Demographically diverse schools were chosen, including schools in the western agricultural communities as well as in urban neighborhoods. Some of the schools were strong performers while others had high populations of "at risk" students with low test scores. Pine Jog's requirements for model schools were:

- that the principal and teachers commit to incorporating an environmental education focus into the curriculum and to allocating funds and teaching planning time to support the project;
- that field experiences in a natural setting are provided for students;
- that teachers participate in professional development with a focus on environmental content and outdoor teaching strategies;
- that teachers work to develop multidisciplinary instructional units with the environment as the unifying theme.

An additional significant feature of the Pine Jog program is that schools have to make a commitment to become financially self-sustaining after a certain amount of time in the program, usually about three years. The idea is for Pine Jog staff to get a school rolling and then move on to work with other schools. Within the first two years, some schools went from receiving 100 percent outside support to just 50 percent by raising other funds to support the program. But while some schools are affluent and can become self-sustaining easily, others struggle to find even minimal funds.

Qualitative and quantitative evaluation of the project shows some interesting results. Students in the third, fourth, and fifth grades in all of the model schools are showing significantly increased achievement in reading, writing, and math on the Florida Writes and the Florida Comprehensive Assessment Tests. The greatest gains in achievement, however, show up in the urban schools with large numbers of minority students and students from groups low on the socioeconomic scale. The study indicates that these findings "further support the educational benefit of experiential education, especially for those student populations that are 'experience-poor.'" (Toth-King and Marcinkowski, 1996)

In other words, Pine Jog's environmental education program makes a greater difference for traditionally low-achieving students, thereby helping to "close the achievement gap" between students in poor communities and those in more prosperous ones.

Other Pine Jog studies have also shown how the program has affected the relationship between the school and the environmental center. Pine Jog is now seen as not just a field trip destination, but as an educational partner for local schools. In addition, Pine Jog staff members are looking beyond traditional options in environmental education professional development and are expressing a desire to attend the Association of Supervision and Curriculum Development (ASCD) and other education-related conferences.

The Gove Elementary School in Belle Glade was one of Pine Jog's model schools in the late 1990s. In the agricultural western part of the county, 70 percent of Gove's student population speaks limited English—Spanish is the most common native language. A large number of students come from migrant farm-worker families. Fourteen percent of the students receive services from the Exceptional Student Education Program, which helps students with challenges ranging from specific learning disabilities to profound mental retardation. Listen to the voices of the past principal and some of the teachers at Gove Elementary describing how their school used place-based education to engage challenged learners:

> At Gove Elementary, both state-mandated reforms and environmental education have had a transforming effect. In 1995, Florida's Commissioner of Education identified Gove as one of 13 "critical schools" in the state whose performance on standardized tests fell far below the national average in reading and math. The school was put on notice to bring up its scores as part of a comprehensive school improvement plan.
>
> Gove's principal, Margarita Pinkos, swiftly made dramatic changes in the way teachers approach their work. At a two-week, voluntary summer retreat last year, she encouraged teachers to collaborate much more, both within and across grade groups. These new perspectives led to a major shift to an integrated curriculum organized around four nine-week themes, and tied to county benchmarks for education.
>
> "Pine Jog taught us a lot about how to create an integrated thematic unit, how you look at benchmarks and tie them in, and how you find meaningful, relevant activities for different learning styles," says Denise

Beaulieu, a speech and language pathologist.

Though many of Gove's teachers have always taught about the environment, the Pine Jog experience cemented their decision to make the environment the focus of one of their school-wide nine-week units. According to Beaulieu and Gayle Zavala, also a speech and language pathologist, the unit offered appropriate learning experiences for all of the students. A group of mentally disabled kindergarten through second grade students cultivated their own garden and wrote about what they grew. A group of fourth graders studied energy through lessons that pulled together several disciplines and incorporated developmentally appropriate literature. To reinforce the new concepts, they read Gary Paulsen's The Tortilla Factory, *in which the lead character—a Mexican farm worker to whom many of the students easily related—follows the different ways energy is used as corn moves from field to factory, store and table.*

The unit culminated with an exciting flourish: the school held an environmental fair in which students in each grade designed activities for the rest of the school to enjoy. At the fourth grade station, students ate nachos baked in a handmade solar oven. A few yards away, second graders fished simulated pollutants, such as oil and miniature tires, out of a model of Lake Okeechobee. Susan Tóth, education director at Pine Jog, said of the fifth graders who created skits and visual aids to teach younger children about cycles: "I was blown away. The fifth graders took their job of teaching the younger kids so seriously." Zavala and Beaulieu say the unit was a success—so successful the school repeated it the following year.

The new approach paid off. Based on standardized test scores, the school was excised from the Commissioner's critical list. (Flanagan, 1999)

The collaboration between Pine Jog and the West Palm Beach County schools illustrates three salient points about place-based education:

1. Programs can be tailored to help schools comply with the demand for increased accountability and test scores. Though these scores are not necessarily the best measure of school effectiveness, the current political climate puts a premium on test scores, and schools must respond. By working hand in hand with schools, administrators, and teachers to raise test scores, Pine Jog demonstrates that the environmental learning center can be a valuable partner in addressing societal concerns rather than just a "Field Trips R Us" service.

2. Place-based education is emerging as a promising model for school improvement. Pine Jog worked conscientiously to help teachers implement their school improvement plan, rather than trying to get them to add environmental curriculum

3. Environmental education and place-based education are particularly well suited to serve the needs of differently-abled children. Children with linguistic disabilities often demonstrate greater competency in visual, spatial, and kinesthetic learning modes. These children learn better when the curriculum is activity-based, concrete, and practical. Using the nearby environment as a vehicle gives these students the grounded experience they need to develop abstract skills. Instead of being marginalized, special-needs students are brought into the mainstream through place-based education.

Place-based education provides a well-provisioned chest of tools that can be used to address a wide range of educational challenges.

Wedding Arts and the Environment in the Bioregional Outdoor Education Project

The Bioregional Outdoor Education Project (BOEP) is a program of the Four Corners School of Outdoor Education, which recently completed its two-year pilot program with four school districts in the Four Corners region of Colorado, Utah, Arizona, and New Mexico.

Have you ever been in the Four Corners region? Picture the most twisted and convoluted landscape on the planet, dotted with tumbling sagebrush and peopled by an odd mixture of river-runners, Navaho, and Mormons. It's an unusual place for a place-based education project because the distances between one school and the next are vast. But the gritty folks at the Four Corners School in Monticello, Utah are taking the bull by the horns and riding it.

> *The mission of the BOEP is to promote understanding and appreciation of the Colorado Plateau through core-based, interdisciplinary, experiential curricula in grades K–6. This innovative program uses a "roving classroom, continuous mentoring" model to deliver teacher training in bioregional education and techniques. (Four Corners School, 2000/01)*

Four Corners School started out as an environmental education program offering river rafting, hiking, and archeological study trips in the Southwest. Over the years they've added a Canyon Country Youth Corps, training programs for eco-educators, and now a program for schools and teachers that tries to send roots deep into the fissures in the sandstone bedrock. Like other environmental centers, they've recognized that they need to make a serious, long-term commitment to raising children who will want to preserve the natural and cultural resources of the Colorado Plateau. In December 2001, Bureau of Land Management offices throughout the region were instructed to speed up the processing of oil and gas well applications from energy companies. With as many as 100,000 new wells slated for the region, it was a good time for a place-based education project. (Kosova, 2002)

Starting with a ten-day, field-based summer institute, BOEP introduces teachers to the concept of bioregion, familiarizes them with the Colorado Plateau, and gives them some preliminary training in place-based curricula and experiential education techniques. A science resource room is created in each school. Then, over a two-year period, BOEP allows the teachers in each participating school, in partnership with Four Corners staff, to co-create the curriculum for their own school, in order to ensure that it addresses the specific needs and mandates of their home districts and states. The finch analogy works here as well—sometimes you need a bigger beak, sometimes you need to change your dietary preference, sometimes you need a slightly different plumage in order to thrive on your home ground.

Having completed its pilot program in one district in each of four states, BOEP is now expanding to another set of schools. Like the Bay Schools and CO-SEED projects, the program utilizes roving educators to help teachers and students bring their curriculum out into the landscape and community. Listen to how two teachers at the Northside Elementary School in Montrose, Colorado, have implemented the program in their classrooms.

Teaching outdoors. Marie Novotny, third grade teacher, describes how she uses the outdoors to meet curriculum requirements:

> *I had the students use the sand play area in our schoolyard to make landforms that they were studying in Social Studies. It helped them*

remember for a test. Another time we used the same sand area to bring out their creativity by making a plan in the sand for a story they would write. The students could use any rocks, sticks, or other materials they found on the playground. Some made decorated stars, some made roads and towns, some small hills with caves in them.... (Later, they wrote the stories that they created in the sand.)

The first of January we studied sound in Science and again went outside and listened to sounds in our area. We thumped on playground equipment and different materials on the playground. They made charts of low sounds, high sounds, and loud and soft sounds. This helped them understand vibrations and why sounds are different.

My students have also enjoyed our mapmaking activities. They made maps to show the way from our school to the park and to the public library. They had to include directions, map keys, street names and landmarks. Then we used the maps to make our way to the park for a sack lunch and another time to the library and on to the Daily Bread for a cookie. We had to use the path they mapped out and notice directions, street signs, and landmarks. We are going out again, soon, to work with compasses and thermometers-—these activities fit our standards for Social Studies and Math. (Four Corners School, 2000/01)

Marie's description nicely illustrates some core principles of place-based education. *First,* she's teaching in the environment rather than about the environment, or to use the jargon, she's using the environment as an integrating context. She's using the sand play area to teach the content of social studies curriculum and to provide prompts for writing experiences. She's using the playground equipment to teach the prescribed science unit on sound.

Second, she's honoring the developmental progression from near to far. Curriculum that follows development from kindergarten through the end of middle school moves from home and school to neighborhood to community to watershed to bioregion to beyond. For third graders, at the neighborhood/community stage, it's just right to be making and using maps to the park and the library.

Third, this is a year-long endeavor. Going outside wasn't unusual; for Marie and her class it became part of the normal flow.

Music in bioregional education. Margaret Freeman, a music teacher at Northside, uses the outdoors to inspire an emotional bond between her students and the natural world:

> *Bioregional education relies on direct experience with nature to create a caring relationship between a student and the natural world. Lessons incorporating the arts can enhance the emotional connection to the outdoors, and give the students techniques to internalize the experience and revisit it at will.*
>
> *This fall we did a Sunrise Song activity in fourth and fifth grade music. The purpose was to encourage a connection with a particular time of day through observation and experience and help children develop an awareness of the cultural significance of the sun....*
>
> *The first class meeting we read the book* The Way to Start a Day *by Byrd Baylor and listened to a recording of a Native American flute piece by R. Carlos Nakai. The students discussed the various ways in which cultures throughout history have welcomed the rising of the sun. Then I explained that the students would be writing their own morning poems or impressions and composing original sunrise songs.*
>
> *The second class time we went outside. The children worked in small groups and wrote their impressions of the morning time. I encouraged quiet observation and writing images using their senses. Some chose to write poetry, some prose, and struggling writers brainstormed lists of words to describe the morning.*
>
> *Next the children chose instruments and began matching their sounds to the writing. I gave the children freedom in this, while they worked within the framework of representing their words in musical sounds. I encouraged sound rather than formal playing technique, and allowed for creativity. Some chose to play only representative sounds, while others composed organized musical pieces.*
>
> *After rehearsal time, we scheduled a performance time. We performed each group's work outside in the morning for the class, teachers, and principal. There was a great variety of work presented, and a lot of reflection from the students on how their music fit in with what they heard and saw in the morning. (Four Corners School, 2000/01)*

Using the arts as an integrative context for learning can be just as valuable as using the environment, and the combination of both can work wonders. Margaret reminds us that enhancing emotional connections with the land is one component of developing a sense of place. In our rush to focus on test scores and frameworks, it's easy to forget that the foundation for good education, the glue, is caring. Remember John Burroughs's guideline "Knowledge without love will not stick. But if love comes first, knowledge is sure to follow." Many of us find it embarrassing to talk about helping students love the land and their community. But, really, isn't that a big piece of what we're all about?

Creating Economic and Environmental Sustainability in the North Coast Rural Challenge Network

The North Coast Rural Challenge Network (NCRCN) is a member of the Rural Schools and Community Trust initiative and is also supported by the Autodesk Foundation, CalServe, and the Center for Ecoliteracy. The project works with elementary, middle, and high schools in four widely separated rural communities in northern California's Mendocino County.

When the North Coast Rural Challenge Network was organized, the big questions on people's minds were:

- How can school reform become a catalyst to revitalize our rural economies?
- How will we sustain our rural quality of life and develop a viable economy that will assure healthy communities for the twenty-first century?

These questions reflect the commitment that unifies all the Rural Schools and Community Trust sites: to consider school improvement and community sustainability as two sides of the same coin. However, the North Coast project is somewhat distinct from the other Rural Trust sites because of its primary goal to foster ecological literacy and a clear connection to the northern California bioregion. And their use of a high-tech fiber optics telecommunications network allows them to transcend the twisting mountain roads that make for an hour or more of travel between each of the four rural towns.

The small school districts included in the North Coast Network— Anderson Valley, Mendocino, Point Arena, and Laytonville—serve large geographical areas that are both culturally and economically diverse.

These schools are the place where everybody comes together—longtime residents and newcomers, loggers, winegrowers and bed and breakfast owners, Anglos, Hispanics and indigenous tribes, high-tech wizards and back to the landers, the wealthy and the poor. In many ways, the community is forged as their kids grow up together in small schools. Linking these districts into a collaborative effort to improve teaching and learning creates a sense of excitement as each town expands its awareness of the possibilities and their ability to learn from one another. (Center for Ecoliteracy, 2000)

Within the first three years of the project beginning, teachers and community members in these four communities implemented more than 125 projects. These ranged from creating scientific research models of local rivers to restoring a historic Chinese temple to examining the potential economic development opportunities provided by a new highway bypass. Network director Ken Matheson reports on the results:

The projects our students have completed take up much more space in our local newspapers than the results of our standardized test scores. Our communities understand and appreciate the educational opportunities we are creating for our children. The state standardized test scores, by the way, have improved in all the NCRCN districts since our project began. (North Coast Rural Challenge Network, 2000)

One striking aspect of many of these projects, especially at the middle and high school levels, is the impact on preserving environmental quality and economic sustainability in the schools and their community. In Laytonville, community coordinator Binet Payne has been one of the driving forces behind a comprehensive school garden with an integrated compost system. Students describe:

We are in our eighth year of our vermicomposting (composting with worms) project and have reduced our district's solid waste by 60–80%. Last year we composted over 2500 pounds of cafeteria food waste in a ten-month period saving the school more than $6,000. We also recycle most of our classroom paper waste, either as bedding for the worms or through the local recycling. (North Coast Rural Challenge Network, 2000)

Remember that the Advanced Placement students in Morrisville, Vermont, estimated that they could recycle up to 80 percent of the school's solid waste and save the school about $5700 per year. The Laytonville figures suggest that these are realistic goals.

In Point Arena, high school students had a chance to make a difference when a local citizen called the school seeking assistance.

A local rancher had decided to sell a parcel of oceanfront land that would invite the development of resort homes and limit public access to some of the best surfing beach for miles around. Citizen Action invited young people to rise to the challenge. Would they like to help build a mile and a half of improved trail to the beach to assure public access for a time? (North Coast Rural Challenge Network, 2000)

Teacher Warren Galletti and a group of students and citizens responded and built the Bluff Trail, a component of a public initiative to buy the land and protect it from real estate development.

Similarly, native plant nurseries have been created in each of the school districts. In Anderson Valley High School in Mendocino, a unique collaboration has led to a school-based business that integrates science and economics education.

A very special school and community partnership has developed in Anderson Valley. Ken Montgomery was the director of the Botanical Gardens south of Fort Bragg for five years while running his own nursery across from Anderson Valley High School. He describes himself as a "plant nerd," familiar with horticulture, botany, and ecology, but the challenge he cared most about was getting Mendocino youth involved in growing native plants and taking an active part in local restoration efforts that would build on the Navarro River Restoration plan.

After a first year of teaching a Native Plants course with science teacher Dick Jordan, the nurseryman said, "I know how to grow plants—that's the easy part—but actually getting contracts and involving students in the restoration work is something else entirely." Students propagated over a thousand plants during the first year while learning botanical and stream restoration concepts. In the second and third year of operation, students...helped community volunteers build the extensive greenhouse facility at the high school in preparation for the creation of a school-based business that provides native plants to land owners.

Ken and the students envisioned a joint venture partnership with the school district. It was clear that they must engage the other science classes at the high school in Anderson Valley and encourage the other school-based greenhouses to consider restoration opportunities, each in its own watershed.

The concept gradually grew to involve the three other NCRCN districts each with their own capacity for growing native plants.

The native plant nursery is now an established school-based business called Mendocino Natives Nursery. Plant sales and grants from the Lebeau Foundation and the National Fish and Wildlife Foundation, provide money to hire a nursery manager and student interns. Funding these positions entirely through plant sales is a realistic goal for the near future.

In addition to growing plants, interns design and maintain a model restoration site on the creek near the school. Students from the science and agriculture classes help with the labor. They have planted, staked and enclosed over 300 young trees with wire mesh to protect them from browsing wildlife while they are still small saplings. This site will demonstrate how native plants can drastically enhance the land and stream and hopefully encourage others to follow suit.

Local landowners are beginning to request growing contracts to propagate native plants, including a rare type of red oak recently identified in Anderson Valley. (North Coast Rural Challenge Network, 2000)

Other economic development initiatives abound in these districts, including a commercial mushroom growing business. School/community business partnerships make for good education and good economic development. Sixth and seventh graders in Antrim, New Hampshire, created a food concession as part of a math/economics business development unit. The students realized that at dozens of school athletic events, no food and drinks were available. They created a business plan, got the permits, did all the buying, kept the books, and made lots of spectators happy. Food from the Hood, a garden products business based in a Los Angeles high school, became a national success a few years ago. And I'm still waiting for an upper elementary or middle school teacher to create a school-based bike shop where students provide bike repair services at a reasonable cost for students and school staff. That's what I would consider developmentally appropriate technology education.

Students and citizens in Mendocino County and across the country are providing vivid models of how to make project-based learning a contributing force in the economic and ecological preservation of their communities. Now it's time to take evolution into your own hands. In Littleton, New Hampshire, high school students and engineers are working on a plan to keep downtown sidewalks snow- and ice-free by piping heated wastewater underneath them. Take that, sprawl America! The capillary oozing of water will keep shoppers downtown and show the world just how ingenious students can be when we harness their energy for the good of the environment and the community. Isn't there a similar project waiting to happen in your neighborhood?

References

Baldwin, Mark. 1998. *Coming Home Conference Proceedings.* Jamestown, NY: Roger Tory Peterson Institute.

Bartsch, Julie. 1999. "School Project Grows to Support Community's Maritime Livelihood." *Rural Matters: The Rural Challenge News* (Winter 1999).

————. 2001. *Community Lessons: Integrating Service Learning into K-12 Curriculum.* Malden, MA: Massachusetts Department of Education.

Bearman, Jessica. 2001. *Bay Schools Project: Year One Report.* Annapolis, MD: Chesapeake Bay Foundation.

Bigelow, Bill. 1996. "How My Schooling Taught Me Contempt for the Earth." *Rethinking Schools* (Fall 1996).

Center for Ecoliteracy. 2000. *Ecoliteracy: Mapping the Terrain.* Berkeley, CA: Center for Ecoliteracy.

Chin, Jack. 2001. *All of a Place: Connecting Schools, Youth and Community.* San Francisco, CA: Bay Area School Reform Collaborative.

Cushman, Kathleen. 1997. "What Rural Schools Can Teach Urban Systems." *Challenge Journal* (The Journal of the Annenberg Challenge) 1, no. 2.

Dewey, John. 1891, 1980. *School and Society.* Carbondale, IL: Southern Illinois University Press.

David Sobel

Dodge, Joe. 2001. Correspondence with author.

Education Development Center. 2000. *Schoolyard Learning: The Impact of Schoolgrounds*. Newton, MA: Education Development Center and the Boston Schoolyard Funders Collaborative.

El Nasser, Haya. 2000. "Old N.H. Town Catches 'Smart Growth' Fever." *USA Today* (15 November).

Flanagan, Ruth. 1999. "Education and the Environment: Partners for Change." *EEducator.* (Publication of the North American Association on Environmental Education), (summer).

Fontaine, Carla. 2000. *School and Community Partnerships: A Model for Environmental Education.* Keene, NH: Antioch New England Institute.

————. 2001. *A Changing Dynamic: The Work of the Community-based School Environmental Education Program.* Keene, NH: Antioch New England Institute.

Four Corners School of Outdoor Education. 2000/01. *Lessons from the Bioregion: Newsletter of the Bioregional Outdoor Education Project 2,* nos. 1, 2, and 3.

Glenn, Joanne L. 2000. *Environment-based Education: Creating High Performance Schools and Students.* Washington, DC: The National Environmental Education and Training Foundation.

Grahn, P. Mårtensson, F. Lindblad, B. Nilsson, P. and A. Ekman. 1997. "Ute på dagis. Hur använder barn daghemsgården?" *Stad & Land* nr 45, Alnarp, Sweden.

Hart, Roger. 1997. *Children's Participation: The Theory and Practice of Involving Young Citizens in Community Development and Environmental Care.* New York, NY: UNICEF.

James, William, letter to Mrs. Henry Whitman, 7 June 1899.

Jorgenson, Robin. 2001. Presentation to the school board at Beebe Environmental and Health Sciences Magnet School, Malden, MA.

Kiefer, Joseph and Martin Kemple. 1998. *Digging Deeper: Integrating Youth Gardens into Schools and Communities.* Montpelier, VT: Common Roots Press.

Kosova, Weston. 2002. "What's Gale Norton Trying to Hide?" *Outside* (June).

Levy, Steven. 1999. *Starting From Scratch.* Portsmouth, NH: Heinemann.

Lieberman, Gerald A. and Linda L. Hoody. 1998. *Closing the Achievement Gap: Using the Environment as an Integrating Context for Learning.* San Diego, CA: State Environment and Education Roundtable.

MacKinnon, Kathleen. 2000. *Report to Congress Assessing Environmental Education in the United States.* Washington, DC: National Environmental Education Advisory Council.

North Coast Rural Challenge Network. 2000. *Exploring Ecoliteracy: Growing a Network of Community-based Learning.* Berkeley, CA: Center for Ecoliteracy.

Null, Elisabeth Higgins. 2002. "East Feliciana Parish Schools Embrace Place-based Education." Rural School and Community Trust website, www.ruraledu.org (March).

Peoples Academy Advanced Placement Environmental Science students. 2001. "Waste Reduction in the Cafeteria at Peoples Academy." Morrisville, VT: Peoples Academy.

Rural Challenge Research and Evaluation Program. 1999. *Living and Learning in Rural Schools and Communities: A Report to the Annenberg Rural Challenge.* Cambridge, MA: Harvard Graduate School of Education.

Smith, Gregory A. and Dilafruz R. Williams. 1999. *Ecological Education in Action: On Weaving Education, Culture and the Environment.* Albany, NY: SUNY Press.

Smith, Gregory A. 2001. "Learning Where We Live." *F2E2 Forum* (a publication of the Funders Forum on Environment and Education), (September).

————. 2002. "Place-based Education: Learning to Be Where We Are At." *Phi Delta Kappan* (April).

Sobel, David. 1996. *Beyond Ecophobia: Reclaiming the Heart in Nature Education.* Great Barrington, MA: The Orion Society.

————. 1999. "Mapping McCabe: Connecting Curriculum and Community through Environmental Education." *Community Works Journal* 4, no. 1.

————. 2001. "You Learn What You Eat: Cognition Meets Nutrition in Berkeley Schools." *Orion Afield* 5, no. 3.

Toth-King, Susan and Tom Marcinkowski. 1996. "Building Environmental Education Programs: A Four Year Evaluative Study." In A. Weiss (Ed.), *Proceedings of the 1995 National Interpreters Workshop.* Ft. Collins, CO: National Association for Interpretation.

Woodhouse, Janice. 2001. "Over the River and Through the Hood: Reviewing Place as a Focus for Pedagogy." *Thresholds in Education* 27, nos. 3 and 4.

Zelezny, Lynnette. 1999. "Educational Interventions That Improve Environmental Behaviors: A Meta-Analysis." *Journal of Environmental Education* 31, no. 1.

Zibart, Rosemary. 2002. "When the Community is the Classroom." *Parade* (28 April).

Additional Readings

Center for Environmental Education. 2001. *Notes from the Field: The CO-SEED Project.* Keene, NH: Antioch New England Institute.

Leslie, Clare Walker, John Tallmadge, and Tom Wessels. 1999. *Into the Field: A Guide to Locally Focused Teaching.* Great Barrington, MA: The Orion Society.

Raffan, James et. al. 2000. *Nature Nurtures: Investigating the Potential of School Grounds.* Toronto, ON: Evergreen Foundation.

Rogers, Laurette. 1994. *The California Freshwater Shrimp Project: An Example of Environmental Project-based Learning.* Berkeley, CA: Heyday Books.

Acknowledgements

Dedicated to my esteemed colleagues Bo Hoppin and Delia Clark, tireless advocates of place-based education. And to the staff of the Antioch New England Institute and the faculty of the Education and Environmental Studies departments at Antioch New England Graduate School who have translated many of these ideas into actuality.

—D.S.

The Orion Society would like to thank the Center for Ecoliteracy, Clements Foundation, and Namaste Foundation for their generous support of this book. We would also like to recognize the early support that the Geraldine R. Dodge Foundation gave to Orion's place-based education work, and to Cristy West for her ongoing support of our educational initiatives. Thanks, as always, to the directors and members of the Myrin Institute for their generosity and vision.

Profound thanks are extended to Dale Abrams, Steve Archibald, Aina Barten, Jack Chin, Amanda Elkin, and Jennifer Sahn for their important editorial contributions to this volume, and Jason Houston and Patrick Kelly for their work on design and production.

About the Author

David Sobel is Director of Teacher Certification Programs in the Education Department at Antioch New England Graduate School. He also co-directs the Community-based School Environmental Education (CO-SEED) program, a place-based education initiative that improves schools, encourages community vitality, and preserves environmental quality in rural and urban communities throughout New England. David is the author of *Children's Special Places, Beyond Ecophobia,* and *Mapmaking with Children* and is a frequent keynote speaker at education and environment conferences. He is working on a new book entitled *A Little Bit of Love between Us and the Trees: Children at Home in the Natural World.* He consults with schools and environmental learning centers to support the greening of educational programs and the evolution of developmentally appropriate science, social studies, and environmental curriculum. He works and plays in the Monadnock Region of southwestern New Hampshire with his children and is committed to year round swimming, the exploration of landscape nooks and crannies, and to joyfully embracing the gift of life on earth.

The ORION Society

The Orion Society's mission is to inform, inspire, and engage individuals and grassroots organizations across North America in becoming a significant cultural force for healing nature and community.

Our programs and publications include:

Orion Magazine
"America's finest environmental magazine" (Boston Globe), is an influential forum for re-imagining humanity's relationship to nature, featuring America's foremost writers and artists.

Orion Grassroots Network
The Orion Grassroots Network connects the full diversity of non-profits engaged in the social and environmental movements of North America and beyond. The member organizations are recognized in their communities as leaders in the fields of conservation, restoration, education, democracy, justice, health, and economics.

Orion Education
Orion encourages place-based, environmental education through publication of books in the Nature Literacy Series and the development of curriculum.

The Orion Society's is a 501(c)3 organization; our programs and publications are made possible in part due to generous donations from individuals, corporations, and philanthropic foundations.

Index

Note: In the index place-based education is abbreviated as PBE. PBE programs are indexed by location.